How the
WHEEL
CHANGED HISTORY

How the WHEEL CHANGED HISTORY

by Melissa Higgins

CONTENT CONSULTANT

John Hoard
Associate Research Scientist
University of Michigan

ESSENTIAL LIBRARY OF
INVENTIONS

Essential Library

An Imprint of Abdo Publishing | abdopublishing.com

abdopublishing.com

Published by Abdo Publishing, a division of ABDO, PO Box 398166, Minneapolis, Minnesota 55439. Copyright © 2016 by Abdo Consulting Group, Inc. International copyrights reserved in all countries. No part of this book may be reproduced in any form without written permission from the publisher. Essential Library™ is a trademark and logo of Abdo Publishing.

Printed in the United States of America, North Mankato, Minnesota
052015
092015

THIS BOOK CONTAINS
RECYCLED MATERIALS

Cover Photos: Shutterstock Images, left, right
Interior Photos: Everett Historical/Shutterstock Images, 2, 52–53, 74–75; L. Prang & Co./Library of Congress, 6–7; Sergey Paranchuk/Shutterstock Images, 9; Florida Center for Instructional Technology, 13; Shutterstock Images, 15, 23, 51 (right); Bettmann/Corbis, 16–17, 69, 71, 72, 96; topten22photo/iStockphoto, 25; iStockphoto, 26–27, 37, 42, 46, 55, 57, 58, 62–63, 70, 79, 83, 89; Peter Visscher/Thinkstock, 32; North Wind Picture Archives, 33; David Thomson/AP Images, 34; Franklin Price Knott/National Geographic Creative/Corbis, 38–39; Toni Flap/iStockphoto, 44; Science & Society Picture Library/Getty Images, 48; Peter Serjeant/Thinkstock, 50; Dorling Kindersley/Thinkstock, 51 (left); Schenectady Museum/Hall of Electrical History Foundation/Corbis, 60; Heritage Images/Corbis, 66; Bill Ragan/Shutterstock Images, 73; Michael Maloney/San Francisco Chronicle/Corbis Images, 77; Corbis, 82; Jia Li/Shutterstock Images, 90–91; Michelin Tweel Technologies, 93; Public Domain, 98

Editor: Susan Bradley
Series Designer: Craig Hinton

Library of Congress Control Number: 2015930961

Cataloging-in-Publication Data

Higgins, Melissa.
 How the wheel changed history / Melissa Higgins.
  p. cm. -- (Essential library of inventions)
Includes bibliographical references and index.
ISBN 978-1-62403-788-7
1. Wheels--History--Juvenile literature.   2. Inventions--Juvenile literature.   I. Title.
621.8--dc23

                                        2015930961

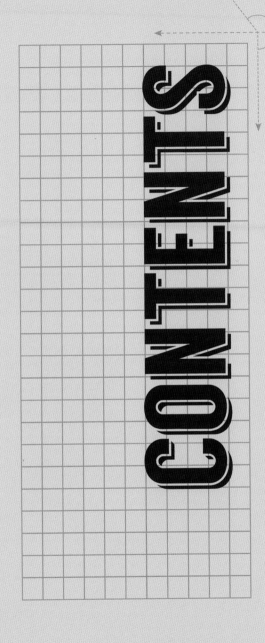

CONTENTS

CHAPTER 1

THE

WHEEL

In 1870s England, bicycles were big—literally big. The front wheel of a high-wheel bicycle could top four feet (1.2 m) in diameter. With its much smaller rear wheel, the metal and wood contraption looked awkward, and it was heavy and difficult to ride. Rigid metal tires made for a bumpy ride, and dismounting from the tall seat was a challenge—and a hazard—even for skilled riders. As noted by American humorist Mark Twain, "Get a bicycle. You will not regret it, if you live."[1] Despite the shortcomings of these ungainly contraptions, they were popular with the rich young men who enjoyed competing with them in bicycle races.

High-wheeled bicycles provided both recreation and transportation for those who were brave enough to ride them.

Tinkering in his Coventry, United Kingdom, workshop, James Starley, a 41-year-old machinist, had no experience building bicycles. But he had a hunch. With only a few improvements, he thought he could make bikes stronger, faster, and more comfortable. First, Starley experimented with a tubular steel frame. Then he made seat springs shorter and stiffer, and he created a rear brake that operated by turning the handlebar grips. But his biggest innovation concerned the front wheel. Spokes on bicycles at the time were stiff and heavy. Starley came up with the idea to stretch wire spokes from the wheel's rim to the hub and then tighten them. Spokes under tension are better at absorbing road shock than rigid spokes are, and they are much lighter.

Starley knew his all-metal Ariel bicycle, which he patented with his partner, William Hillman, in 1870, was a big improvement from earlier high wheelers. But he needed a way to show bicycle enthusiasts what the Ariel could do. In 1871, Starley and Hillman rode their Ariel bicycles from London to Coventry in one day—a 100-mile (161 km) trip on primitive roads. Both men were so exhausted that they stayed in bed for the next three days, but the publicity stunt worked. They gained as one of their first customers James Moore, a famous racing cyclist.

The Ariel became popular and sold well. Even so, Starley had a feeling he could make more improvements, and he continued working on spoke technology. In 1874, he introduced the tangent-spoke wheel. The load-bearing principle was the same as for his previous tension wheel. But in this new Ariel, he connected the spokes from the rim to the hub at an angle, rather than in a straight line. Tangent spokes were very strong and could better withstand the forces of pedaling and braking than straight spokes could. The result was a wheel that was even lighter and better riding than it was before. Starley's innovation was such a success that nearly every bike built since 1874 has used this technology. Tangent spokes have even been used on motorcycle, car, and airplane wheels.

Because of his innovations and the fact his Ariel bike marked the beginning of Britain's bicycle manufacturing industry, Starley earned the title "father of the bicycle industry." Bike historian Andrew Ritchie says Starley was "probably the most energetic and inventive genius in the history of bicycle technology."[2]

Trains, Planes, and Dishwashers

It is hard to imagine the present-day world without the wheel. Wheels are integral to

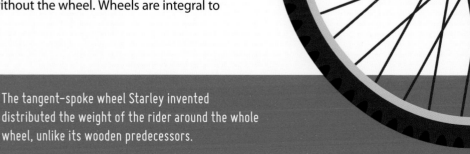

The tangent-spoke wheel Starley invented distributed the weight of the rider around the whole wheel, unlike its wooden predecessors.

THE ROOT OF IT ALL

The word *wheel* comes from the root word *wegh*, which means "to convey, particularly by a wheeled vehicle" in the ancient language from which it is believed all Indo-European languages derived.[3] In Old English, the word became *hweol*. Because the root word for *wheel* can be found in almost every offshoot of the original Proto-Indo-European language, this means wheels and wheeled vehicles were around when the language was last used approximately 6,000 years ago.

transportation—cars, trucks, trains, planes, motorcycles, wagons, farm equipment, skateboards, and, of course, bicycles, would not function without them. But wheels are not only used for transportation. Practically every machine uses a spinning disc of some sort. Wheels can be found in everything from computer disc drives to clocks, electric toothbrushes, and dishwashers.

Although wheels are widely used now, they were invented relatively late in human history. People were already forming societies, herding domesticated animals, and farming during the Bronze Age when the wheel first appeared. The first wheels were not even used for transportation. Archaeological evidence indicates the very first wheels may have been attached to children's toys. Probably the earliest functional use of the wheel was for making pottery. The timesaving, product-improving pottery wheel would serve as inspiration for countless wheeled machines that came after it.

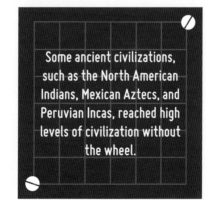

Some ancient civilizations, such as the North American Indians, Mexican Aztecs, and Peruvian Incas, reached high levels of civilization without the wheel.

From the Human Mind

Many human inventions are inspired by nature. The hook-and-loop fastener used on everything from sneakers to spacesuits was created after Swiss inventor Georges de Mestral noticed how plant burrs attached to his dog's fur during walks in the woods. Certainly the airplane was inspired by people's observation of birds in flight. In the case of wheels, however, there were no known examples of wheels in nature at the time they first came into use. Wheels were truly an invention that sprang from the human mind.

So in whose mind was the wheel conceived? Unlike Thomas Edison's light bulb or Gottlieb Daimler's gas-powered automobile, the name of the wheel's inventor—or possibly many inventors in different parts of the world—is not known. Although the skills needed to build wheels existed in both Europe and the Near East, the first evidence of a wheeled vehicle is a pictograph of a wheeled sled made in approximately 3500 BCE in Mesopotamia, part of modern-day Iraq. Pottery remnants from this era found in southern Poland also contain representations of a

WHEELED BACTERIA

Some single-celled bacteria have an interesting way of getting around—a flagellum. An organic rotating engine drives the long, whiplike flagellum. The engine, powered by protein, is anchored to the cell wall and drives the flagellum, rotating it at up to 100 times per second. The flagellum allows the bacteria cell to move and change direction.

four-wheeled wagon. Wherever the first wheels were made, the technology spread rapidly between 3400 and 3000 BCE.

On a Roll

Other than minor improvements, such as spokes, sectioned rims, and metal tires, vehicle wheels remained relatively unchanged for thousands of years until the Industrial Revolution and the invention of the pneumatic tire in the 1800s. But machines that used wheels or wheel-like devices, such as gears and moving discs, were on a roll from the very beginning. If there was a way the wheel could make a task easier and improve life, there was an inventor ready to take advantage of it.

Wheeled vehicles and machines make tasks easier, and they have improved everyday life in many ways. It is not an exaggeration to say the wheel changed the world. Wheeled grain mills produced more and more food. Better and more abundant pottery increased storage capacity for that food. Wheeled carts, capitalizing on the strength of domesticated animals such as horses and oxen, carried heavier and greater quantities of food and goods longer distances in shorter periods. Spinning wheels spun thread to clothe the ever-increasing population eating the bread made from all that grain. In time, the laborsaving benefits of the wheel freed people from having to devote all their

LEVER **WHEEL AND AXLE** **PULLEY**

INCLINED PLANE **WEDGE** **SCREW**

These six machines comprise the building blocks with which all complex machines are made. They serve a useful purpose by changing the strength or direction of a force.

energy to survival, enabling them to pursue education, arts, and other creative endeavors. Improvements brought by the wheel made it possible for civilization to expand in countless ways.

SIX BASIC MACHINES

The wheel is one of six basic machines: the lever, wheel with axle, pulley, inclined plane, wedge, and screw. All simple machines create more force than is put into them by transferring or amplifying the initial force. Force applied to a wheel (for example, wind moving a windmill's blades) magnifies the rotation of the axle. Force applied to an axle (such as from a car's gasoline engine) magnifies the rotation of the wheel. Simple machines have been used for thousands of years in various forms. The term *mechanical advantage* indicates the ratio of the output force to the input force. For example, looping a rope over a barn rafter and pulling on it to lift a heavy object creates a favorable mechanical advantage compared with lifting the object unaided.

FUN WHEELS

The most useful wheeled inventions help people move and make things. But wheels also provide entertainment. A good example is the Ferris wheel. Called "pleasure wheels" when they first came into use throughout Europe in the 1600s, the large wooden wheels with hanging seats were turned by strong men. American engineer George Washington Gale Ferris Jr. built the first steam-powered "big wheel" for the 1893 World's Columbian Exposition in Chicago, Illinois. At 264 feet (80 m) tall, Ferris designed it to rival France's Eiffel Tower. Ferris's machine could carry 2,160 people in 35 hanging gondolas.[5] An even taller machine was built for the 1895 Empire of India exhibition, which had more than 2.5 million visitors during its 12-year run.[6] In 1896, the machine's operator paid riders the equivalent of several months' wages after a mishap forced them to dangle in midair all night. One of the tallest modern Ferris wheels is the 541-foot- (165 m) tall Singapore Flyer, which features 28 air-conditioned capsules.[7]

As it did for Starley, the wheel has inspired many inventors to make improvements to existing wheeled machines or to create something entirely new. Said Robert Fulton, inventor of the first practical steamboat, "The mechanic should sit down among levers, screws, wedges, wheels, etc. like a poet among the letters of the alphabet, considering them as the exhibition of his thoughts; in which a new arrangement transmits a new idea to the world."[4] Although today the wheel and the countless inventions it spawned may be taken for granted, its history is anything but ordinary.

TIMELINE
THE WHEEL

ca. 3500 BCE
The first-known potter's wheel is used in Mesopotamia.

ca. 3300 BCE
Four-wheeled wagons are used in Europe.

ca. 2000 BCE
Chariots are used for war in Europe, North Africa, and the Middle East.

ca. 400– 300 BCE
The Greeks develop cogs, gears, and pulleys.

ca. 80 BCE
The waterwheel is used in the eastern Mediterranean region.

500– 1000 CE
The spinning wheel is developed in China.

1803
Englishman Richard Trevithick builds the first successful steam railroad locomotive.

1807
American Robert Fulton builds the first practical waterwheel steamboat.

1817
German Baron von Drais invents the first bicycle.

1885
German Karl Benz builds a four-wheeled, gasoline-engine car.

1887
Scotsman John Dunlop develops the pneumatic tire, originally designed for a bicycle.

1908
The first mass-produced automobile, the Model T Ford, comes off the assembly line in the United States.

1930
English engineer Frank Whittle invents the gas-turbine jet engine.

1956
IBM introduces the first computer-disc storage system.

1997
NASA lands its Sojourner rover on Mars to explore the planet's surface.

15

CHAPTER 2

WHY THE WHEEL?

A possible explanation for the relatively late arrival of the wheel in human history is that for a long time, the climate and terrain of the earth were not well suited for rolling things. Until the end of the last Ice Age in approximately 10,000 BCE, ice sheets covered nearly one-third of the earth.[1] Bogs, sandy deserts, or jungles, all of which were unfavorable terrain for wheels, covered other land. In addition, early people were so busy hunting game and gathering plants in order to feed, clothe, and shelter themselves that they had little time or energy to contemplate inventions such as the wheel.

According to some historians, the precursor of the wheel was a log. A flat surface resting on logs allowed objects to be pulled rather than carried.

WHEELS IN THE NEW WORLD

A major puzzle for historians is that the advanced civilizations of the Americas did not use wheels for transportation even though they made use of wheels on pull toys for children. One theory is that the widespread use of slave labor made the wheel unnecessary for hauling. However, slave labor was also used in Mesopotamia, Sumer, and Egypt, where the wheel was regularly employed. Another explanation is that draft animals did not exist in the New World. Although llamas and alpacas were domesticated by 3500 BCE, they were used mostly as pack animals. There were no horses, oxen, or cattle in the Western Hemisphere to aid in pulling. In addition, wheeled vehicles were nearly useless in dense Amazon jungles and the rugged Andean mountains. Still, the wheelbarrow and potter's wheel could have been useful in local areas. The puzzle remains.

In approximately 7000 BCE, people began domesticating animals and harvesting and storing food. They settled down into villages and stayed in one place, particularly in the temperate areas of the world, such as Mesopotamia, Egypt, and parts of China. Struggling less for daily survival, people had enough free time to begin thinking about ways to improve their lives—such as how to more easily make a clay pot or move a heavy load of grain.

What Came before the Wheel?

The earliest method of transporting goods was human muscle power. Using packs and head straps, people carried loads on their backs or pulled objects directly along the

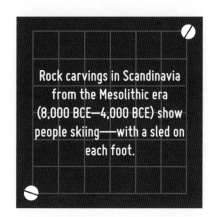

Rock carvings in Scandinavia from the Mesolithic era (8,000 BCE–4,000 BCE) show people skiing—with a sled on each foot.

ground. Once animals were domesticated, someone realized an ox could carry and pull much more weight than a person could. Using human power or beast power, European farmers dragged and carried manure to their fields and returned from their fields with harvested crops. They hauled firewood, construction materials, hides, and clay for making pottery. If a load was extremely heavy, the only way to move it was on water using rafts or on land using groups of men or animals dragging the load.

Sleds made of wooden logs or reeds were a later invention that did a better job of dragging objects too heavy to lift. A sled's smooth bottom created less friction and did not catch so easily on brush and rocks. Some sleds had completely flat bottoms, whereas others had two runners that reduced the amount of contact with the ground even more effectively. The sled, also known as a sledge, worked particularly well in areas with snow, ice, or sand.

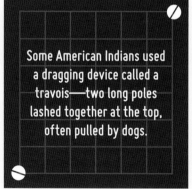

Some American Indians used a dragging device called a travois—two long poles lashed together at the top, often pulled by dogs.

The Beginning of an Idea

Some historians believe the idea for the wheel resulted from people pushing or pulling sleds over a row of logs. The last log would be moved from the back to the front of the load once the sled had passed over it. According to this theory, the sled's runners started to wear down parts of the logs, making grooves. The grooves created a

WHEEL AND AXLE ORIGINS

Historians who support the theory of wheels evolving from logs suggest users decreased their workload through the development of primitive carts. It was more efficient to push or pull a wheel on an axle than to push a heavy sled or log.

one-piece wheel and axle combination that was more stable and efficient at moving the load than only a log. In time, to reduce the effort required to push the logs and to minimize friction with the ground, historians speculate craftsmen carved away part of the log between the grooves. The result was a log shaped much like a modern-day barbell. From there, historians theorize wooden pegs were inserted through the sled in front of and behind the grooved log to hold it in place. In this way, using multiple logs was no longer necessary, and the first wheeled cart was born.

Other historians believe evidence of the log-roller theory is not conclusive. They point to the earliest evidence of wheels from Mesopotamia, where few large trees grew. Also, it would have been difficult to roll whole logs on uneven terrain, and because wood is strongest when it is cut crosswise to the grain, even thick logs would not have held up with time when heavy loads were set on top of them. Unless definitive archaeological evidence is found, the early origins of the wheel may never be known.

The Wheel's Physical Advantage

However the first wheel came about, its advantages must have been quickly apparent. The laws of physics dictate that wheels are simply better at moving objects than sleds are because they typically provide an advantage in countering friction. When a sled drags across

PARTS OF A VEHICLE WHEEL

- Axle—Rod or spindle that passes through the center of a wheel and attaches to the main body of a vehicle.
- Bearing—A machine part in which another part turns or slides.
- Hub—Center part of a wheel through which the axle is inserted.
- Spokes—Bars that connect a wheel's hub to the rim.
- Rim—Circular outer part of a wheel, usually joined to the hub by spokes.
- Tire—Wooden, metal, or rubber cushion that fits around the rim of a wheel to protect the wheel and/or soften the ride.
- Linchpin—Locking pin inserted crossways in an axle to keep the wheel attached to the axle.

SLEDS AND THE PYRAMIDS

To move stones that were 2.5 to 15 short tons (2.3 to 13.6 metric tons) up a rising pyramid, historians believe ancient Egyptian builders used ramps with a gentle incline.[2] The giant blocks were hauled up the ramps on sleds by means of rope pulleys. Wheeled carts were not an option owing to the massive weight of the stones. Constructing a pyramid required a huge workforce of between 10,000 and 100,000 people. These workers are not thought to have been slaves, as there is evidence of thriving communities at the worksites.

the ground, there is friction along its entire length. Except in rare circumstances, wheels allow easier movement because rolling friction is less than sliding friction. As a result, the same load can be moved with considerably less effort on a cart than on a sled.

Another reason the wheel works is because it acts like a lever. When a wheel turns on its rim, the force exerted on the axle is multiplied. A good illustration of this concept is a ship captain's wheel: turning the outside of the wheel causes the center of the wheel to turn more slowly, but with a greater amount of force. The increase in force caused by leverage more than offsets the loss of energy through friction at the hub.

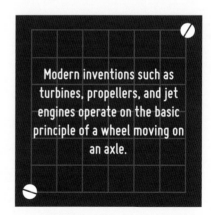

Modern inventions such as turbines, propellers, and jet engines operate on the basic principle of a wheel moving on an axle.

A rotating wheel acts as a lever. When a certain amount of force is applied to turn the wheel's rim, that force is multiplied at the axle.

The Wheel's Social Advantage

The two-wheeled cart revolutionized farming. Prior to the use of wheeled vehicles, farms fanned out from small villages. Groups of farmers would go to the fields and haul fertilizer, seeds, and planting tools on their backs or with sleds. At the end of the growing season, they would carry or drag the harvested crops back to the village. The more

WHEEL AS SYMBOL

The wheel not only found its way into vehicles and machinery, it also became a religious and spiritual symbol. In Buddhism, the wheel came to represent the endless cycle of karma and rebirth. It shows the three basic areas of Buddhist practice — the hub as moral discipline, the spokes as wisdom, and the rim as concentration. In the Middle Ages in Europe, the Wheel of Life came to represent the cyclical nature of life's fortunes by showing a human figure rolling from happiness to loss, suffering, and finally hope. The Native American medicine wheel, sometimes known as the Sacred Hoop, has been used by many native peoples to foster health and healing through balance in life. The four segments of the wheel alternatively represent compass directions, stages of life, seasons, or natural elements such as plants, animals, or the sky.

prosperous farming groups had domesticated oxen and cattle to help with these transportation and planting chores.

The introduction of the wheeled cart enabled single-family farming, as large groups of people were no longer needed to haul materials. This allowed farmers to spread out and use more distant land for food production. Historians believe that the decline of communal villages and the rapid spread of family farms throughout Europe after 3500 BCE were the result of the introduction of the wheel.

The wheel and cart had a similar, if slightly different, effect on the people of the Eurasian grasslands and steppes. The economy in this area depended more on herding animals than on farming. People needed to stay near streams and rivers so their animals would have access to water. The wheeled cart enabled herders to more easily transport their tents, water, and food far into the plains so they could follow their animals as they grazed and drank. Traveling farther into interior grasslands, humans

Domesticated animals, when combined with wheeled vehicles, transformed the nature of farming in the ancient world. Individual families could do more work with fewer people.

expanded into new areas, eventually making contact with their previously unknown neighbors to the west. So among its other accomplishments, the wheel kept the spread of civilization rolling along.

CHAPTER 3

CREATING THE FIRST
WHEEL

A rchaeologists are not sure exactly where the wheel and axle combination originated. Most experts speculate the earliest wheeled vehicles came from Mesopotamia. The area is considered more urban and sophisticated than other parts of the world, and early pictographs depict sleds with wheels. But the sleds of northern European tribal societies also could have served as models. In 2002, archaeologists in Slovenia uncovered the remains of a wooden wheel dated to approximately 3150 BCE based on radiocarbon dating. Whether the wheel and axle originated in Mesopotamia or the Eurasian steppes, there is abundant evidence

The earliest wooden wheels were formed by joining several pieces of wood together, as they were stronger than those made from the cross section of a log.

EARLY EVIDENCE OF WHEELS IN EUROPE

Archaeologists uncovered a clay mug depicting a four-wheeled wagon, harness pole, and yoke in southern Poland and dated it to between 3500 and 3350 BCE. It is the oldest two-dimensional image of a wagon whose age has been confirmed through radiocarbon dating. The oldest three-dimensional model of a wagon was found in eastern Hungary, dated to 3300 to 3100 BCE. Remains of actual wagons, believed to have been used as funeral vehicles, were found in burial mounds in the steppe grasslands of Russia and Ukraine. They were dated to approximately 3000 to 2000 BCE. One of these wagons was 3.8 feet (1.2 m) wide and 6.6 feet (2 m) long.[1]

of rapidly spreading wagon technology throughout Europe and the Near East between 3500 and 3000 BCE.

The First Wheels

Large trees were hard to find in the Middle East, so builders in Mesopotamia constructed wheels from separate planks of wood secured with two or more wooden crosspieces. Later, in tree-rich northern Europe, Scandinavians built wheels out of single slabs of wood.

Although inventing the wheel was ingenious, the wheel itself was not the most difficult part of getting vehicles rolling. The hard part was figuring out how to attach the wheel to a flat-bedded sled or sledge. The solution was the axle. Although it seems obvious now, the earliest wheels and axles must have been anything but obvious.

Attaching an axle and two wheels to a cart was accomplished in two ways. In one, the cart maker firmly attached the wheels to the axle so that the wheels and axle turned at the same time. Before fastening the wheels to the axle, the cart maker inserted the axle through holes in wooden pieces that extended from the bottom of the cart. The axle and wheel combination could then turn inside these holes as the cart was pulled along. This method worked fine for traveling forward and backward, but when turning a corner, the wheels dragged and skipped because the outer wheel had to travel farther than the inner wheel. Cart makers overcame this problem through the second way, which was to attach the axle to the cart as before but allow the wheels to spin independently on the axle. They achieved this free movement by drilling a hole in the center of each wheel, inserting the axle through it, and

WHEELBARROW

Essentially a one-wheeled cart, the wheelbarrow was an important invention, as it allowed a single worker to move a much heavier load than could be carried by hand or on one's back. The wheelbarrow originated in China before 100 CE but did not appear in Europe until much later. A stained-glass window at Chartres Cathedral in France, dated approximately 1220, depicts an early European wheelbarrow.

securing it with a linchpin. In both scenarios, there was quite a bit of friction where the moving parts met. Because wooden parts did not wear well, cart makers experimented with sheathing the axles and lining the wheel hubs with copper and bronze to form a bearing.

Another complication cart makers faced was that the wheel, axle, and hub needed to be nearly perfectly round for everything to fit tightly and not wobble. In fact, some historians believe the need for roundness is another reason why the wheel was developed relatively late in human history—the copper chisels and gouges needed to cut holes and axle ends were not developed until the Bronze Age, which began after 4000 BCE.

Early Wheeled Vehicles

The first wheels were solid, heavy, and clumsy, and they made for a very bumpy ride. Further, the wood wore unevenly and tended to split. Nonetheless, solid wheels worked well enough that it took nearly 1,500 years for someone to come up with an improvement—spokes and rims made from separate pieces of wood. This combination was much lighter than solid wooden wheels, but proved to be just as strong. Crude spoke wheels began appearing in Mesopotamia by 2000 BCE, in Egypt by 1600 BCE, in China by 1300 BCE, and in Scandinavia by 1000 BCE.

Evidence indicates that by approximately 2000 BCE, wheel makers began wrapping copper over the rims to protect them, resulting in the first tires. It would be much later, in the 1760s, that the first continuous metal tire was used. A wheel maker would heat a hoop of iron, sized somewhat smaller than the wooden wheel rim. The hoop would expand in the heat, the wheel maker would fit it around the rim, and as the iron cooled, it shrank to tightly grip the wheel. Metal tires allowed for lighter, stronger, and thinner wheels.

The earliest wheeled vehicles were two-wheeled carts pulled by oxen and used for hauling goods. Later, as animal yokes improved, drivers used horses as well as oxen. With improved yokes and speedy horses, the military transformed the cart into a chariot—the first wheeled machine of war. The chariot was light, fast, and maneuverable, revolutionizing warfare. By 2000 BCE, the chariot and the bow and arrow had come to define military might. War chariots were used across the Middle East, North Africa, and Europe. Then, during the time of Alexander the Great, in approximately 340 BCE, the chariot lost favor, as men could move faster and more nimbly on horseback.

Although use of the chariot as a war machine waned, its use in transportation continued. Egyptian rulers reserved chariots for their own

YOKES

Early wheeled carts varied in how they were made, but they had one thing in common—a long pole to which draft animals were attached. The first animals successfully used to pull carts were oxen. They were attached to the pole with a yoke, a crossbar attached to the pole. The oxen pushed against the bar with their broad shoulders. Horses did not fare as well with this type of yoke because it restricted their breathing and blood flow. Horses were used for lighter work until the Middle Ages, when horse harnesses were developed. Yokes were unknown in the New World. Only dogs and llamas had been domesticated before the arrival of Europeans in the 1500s, and neither was suited for heavy work as draft animals.

ULTIMATE CHARIOT

Persians built an eight-horse chariot in approximately 200 BCE. It had blades attached to the wheels to shred nearby foot soldiers. These chariots were driven fast and could easily overtake soldiers on foot. They provided a solid platform for archers to shoot arrows at their enemies.

use. The Greeks and Romans used them for racing; in fact, chariot racing was included as an event in the early Olympic Games. Many merchants in Rome traveled in chariots where both driver and passenger stood on a platform that was open in the back. Wealthy Greek men and women rode seated in small chariots. Chariots with wheels and axles made entirely of iron or bronze were used in Greece around 250 BCE.

Not only did chariots change with time, so, too, did the four-wheeled cart. In Rome, four-wheeled wagons were used for both ceremonial purposes and for hauling heavy commercial loads. As roads improved and cities grew, members of the general public used wheeled vehicles to travel, including for longer distances. In England during the 1600s, public coaches traveled in stages (thus the origin of the word *stagecoach*) with drivers adding fresh horses at each

Superior chariot design allowed the Hittite people (1400—1200 BCE) to expand their empire in Asia Minor.

Using vehicles for public transport brought a new problem to the English countryside: highway robbery. Highwaymen viewed solitary, unprotected coaches and their occupants as easy prey.

stage. Early four-wheeled transport was bumpy and uncomfortable. By the early 1700s, wagon makers were adding leather and metal springs to make wheeled travel more bearable.

For thousands of years, the basic spoke and rim configuration remained basically unchanged. But similar to modern cars, wagons' and coaches' exteriors changed, sometimes dramatically—from sporty two-wheel curricles to

lavish coaches. The royal coach of King George III of England, first put into service in 1762, weighed 4.8 short tons (4 metric tons) and needed eight horses to pull it.[2] The coach, which is adorned with intricately painted panels and gold leaf, is still driven for royal processions today.

With Wheels Came Roads

With wheeled vehicles came the need for flat and smooth surfaces to drive on. Roads first appeared between 3000 and 2000 BCE but were no more than dirt tracks. Roads of varying quality were built from Italy to Denmark by 2000 BCE. The Silk Road, a series of trails and roads used for trade, connected Rome and China by 100 BCE.

The Romans built durable, well-engineered roads, using flat and crushed stones as pavement, sometimes piled three feet (1 m) deep to withstand rainwater and heavy use by troops. Modern roads, in comparison, are usually half that deep. Beginning in 312 BCE, Roman roads eventually stretched across the expansive Roman Empire, including in Greece, Spain, the North African coast, France, Britain, and much of the Middle East. At its peak, there were more than 50,000 miles (80,000 km) of roads in the

In England during the 1700s, guards would charge a toll to enter a roadway. When they were paid, they would turn aside a long pike or lance to allow passage—hence, the word *turnpike* came to refer to a highway.

This gilded coach owned by the British monarchy has been used at every coronation since King William IV in 1831.

NOT FIT FOR THE DESERT

Between 100 and 500 CE, camels replaced wheeled carts as the main mode of transportation in the deserts of North Africa and the Middle East. Some historians believe this is because cart travel became difficult after the end of the Roman Empire when roads fell into disrepair. Historians have also conjectured that the camel saddle, invented between 500 and 100 BCE, allowed camels to carry loads more comfortably. Camels could travel farther and with less water than cart-pulling oxen. Wheels in this region continued to be used for irrigation, milling, and making pottery.

Roman Empire.[3] Although the Romans originally built roads for travel by couriers and tax collectors, the routes enabled merchants to expand trade and made it possible for people of different cultures to exchange ideas. Roman roads also afforded a quick way to transport soldiers to outlying trouble spots or to conquer neighboring territories.

Roman-built roads fell into disuse with the fall of the Roman Empire by the late 400s, and it was not until the 1700s that road building returned to a similar level of engineering. The first modern road in Europe was the famed Champs-Elysees in Paris, paved with asphalt in 1824. During the remainder of the century, well-drained and waterproofed roads became widespread throughout Europe. Roads in the United States began catching up by the early 1900s. Asphalt and concrete now make for strong and durable roads in many parts of the world.

The Appian Way, built in 312 BCE, was a strategic Roman road connecting Rome to southeast Italy. Portions of the road are still visible today.

CHAPTER 4

EARLY WHEELED MACHINES

A s important as the wheel was to transportation, it was equally important to the advent of machines. As with the wheel, no one is sure who invented most of the early machines that took advantage of the wheel's rotational force. It is likely workers invented these machines to simplify and speed their tasks. As fewer and fewer people were needed to make pottery, grind grain, or make thread, they were free to pursue other occupations or enjoy leisure time.

A primitive potter's wheel made it easier for a potter to add coils to pots and smooth the sides of the pots while working.

Potter's Wheel

By approximately 3500 BCE, potters in Mesopotamia were using simple turntables to make smooth-sided pots from clay. Potters were highly revered at the time, and pottery making was a skilled craft. To make pottery, a potter would coil or mold clay by hand. To make the sides as smooth and even as possible, the potter either had to turn the pot or move himself or herself around it. Because turning the pot took less effort, it is easy to understand how a potter might have imagined a rotating disc helping with the task.

The first potter's wheels were turned by hand. Eventually, they were adapted to be turned by foot with a kick wheel. Late in the Early Bronze Age, by approximately 2400 BCE, the potter's wheel was in wide use. Potter's wheels allowed potters to make better quality pottery more quickly and with less effort. They may have served as inspiration for other wheeled machines as well.

Waterwheel

All machines need power to operate. In ancient times, that power came from the muscles of humans or animals. The first energy source that didn't rely on muscle power was water. Historians believe the waterwheel was first used in the eastern Mediterranean region in

> Goths attacking Rome in 537 CE destroyed waterways that powered grain mills. To ensure a supply of flour, Roman general Belisarius mounted waterwheels between boats to power grain-grinding machines.

THE SAWMILL

Turning logs into lumber by hand was a labor-intensive process. It required two men working with a two-handed saw in a sawpit. One man stood above the log, the other below. Together, they sawed the length of the log. It was difficult, time-consuming, and dusty work, particularly for the sawyer (usually an apprentice) in the bottom of the pit. In 1204, the first water-powered sawmill was built in France, turning this once-tedious task into a much simpler and quicker process. To harness the waterpower, a vertical saw was hung in a wooden frame, with the lower end of the saw blade attached to the waterwheel by a crank. When the rushing water spun the wheel, the crank turned and caused the saw blade to move up and down. At the same time, waterpower spun a large gear that propelled the log into the saw blade. One man operating this kind of sawmill could produce as much lumber in a day as two men working by hand for a week.

approximately 80 BCE. Roman records dating to 18 BCE indicate the use of waterwheels for grinding grain. By 300 CE, Roman flour mills equipped with several wheels were processing tons of grain every day and feeding an ever-growing population. In addition to grinding grain, early waterwheels lifted water to irrigate fields and were later used to cut stone and wood.

Waterwheels work by transferring the energy of moving water to machines. A large wheel rimmed with paddles or buckets is situated over swiftly moving water, such as a river or stream. Or, in another method, the wheel is placed downhill from water directed to it from above. The moving water pushes the paddles or buckets, thus moving the wheel. A horizontal rod attached to the wheel's hub rotates, turning a series of cogged gears, which then rotate a vertical rod. In the case of a grain mill, the vertical rod is attached to a large circular stone called a millstone that rotates

over a stationary millstone placed beneath it. Grain is placed between the two stones, grinding it into flour.

Windmill

Not every area of the ancient world had access to swiftly flowing streams or rivers. But they did have another source of non-muscle energy: wind. Remains of windmills dating back to 700 BCE have been found in Persia and Mesopotamia.

Windmills operate essentially the same as waterwheels, with rods and a series of gears. But rather than paddles or buckets that catch water, windmills' blades catch the wind. Early windmills needed to be adjustable so they could be turned to face the wind. At first, the entire windmill had to be turned, which required the structure to be small and lightweight. Later advancements allowed the miller to turn only the cap to which the blade and hub structure was attached. This allowed for the construction of sturdy, tall windmills that could capture even more wind. Like their water-powered counterparts, windmills were used to grind grain and pump water. Later, they powered sawmills,

ROMAN WATERWHEEL COMPLEX

Between 200 and 300 CE in southern France, the Romans built a complex of 16 waterwheels powering 32 flour millstones. The wheels produced 30 short tons (27 metric tons) of flour per day, enough to feed 10,000 people. This complex was estimated to generate from 30 to 32 horsepower (22 to 24 kw).[1] It was the most powerful mechanical installation in the world for 1,500 years until the steam engine became widely used in the late 1700s.

Water, the first renewable energy source to be harnessed by humans, made it possible to meet the food demands of a growing world population.

ground spices, turned wood pulp into paper, and pulverized chalk and paint pigments.

By producing greater quantities of grain more rapidly, waterwheels and windmills increased food production, allowing populations to grow. Changing grinding into a less labor-intensive chore freed at least some people to pursue a broader range of occupations and express their creativity in more fulfilling ways.

Spinning Wheel

At approximately the same time millers were grinding grain using water and wind power in Europe and the Middle East, cloth makers in Asia were taking advantage of another wheel-based invention: the spinning wheel. In ancient times, yarn was made by attaching raw cotton or wool to a long, weighted stick. The yarn maker would twirl the stick while teasing out a strand of cotton or wool. This twisting and pulling action created a length of coarse thread.

Windmills automated the process of grinding grain.

As trade grew among regions of the world, the demand for silk fabric increased. Chinese silk spinners invented the spinning wheel to help them work with the long, tough secretions of silkworms used to make thread.

Between 500 and 1000 CE, the Chinese began using spinning wheels for making yarn, and by the 1200s, spinning wheels began appearing in Europe. Spinning wheels simplified the spinning process by employing a large vertical wheel. The spinner would turn the wheel with one hand, and with the other hand feed wool or cotton into a groove on the rim of the wheel. Later developments included using a foot pedal as the power source to free up the spinner's hands.

Clocks and Watches

In ancient times, people used burning candles, sticks of incense, trickling water, sand passing through glass bulbs, and the angle of the sun to tell time. Descriptions of water clocks called clepsydras were found in an Egyptian tomb dating to 1500 BCE. All of these methods had disadvantages, such as needing sunlight or requiring constant monitoring of a burning candle or hourglass.

The origin of the word *clock* is *glock*, a German word meaning "bell." Early German clocks had no hands or dials. A chiming bell told the time.

The first use of the wheel in timekeeping came in 725 CE, when Chinese engineer Liang Ling-Zan and Buddhist monk Yi-Xing made the first mechanical clock. The clock used a giant paddlewheel made of cups. As a cup filled with water, it turned the wheel one thirty-sixth of a turn. The clock told the time of the day, the day of the year, and the phase of the moon. In approximately 1090, Chinese imperial minister Su Sung constructed a 30-foot- (9 m) tall water-driven clock that also showed the

movements of the stars. Called the Cosmic Engine, it ran for more than 130 years, stopping only when an invading army seized it and was unable to restart it.[2]

Around 996, the French cleric Gerbert of Aurillac, who would later become Pope Sylvester II, invented a clock powered by a slowly falling weight. In 1502, German clockmaker Peter Henlein invented a spring-driven clock. And in 1656, Christiaan Huygens, a Dutch scientist, designed the first pendulum clock. The chronometer, a timekeeping device used in marine navigation, came into use in the 1700s. It was designed to keep accurate time even on a moving ship or with changes in temperature, humidity, or air pressure.

In all mechanical clocks, power gears take energy from the spring or falling weight and drive the clock mechanism at the right speed. Timekeeping gears, which are usually finer and more precisely made than power gears, drive the hands around the clock face at different speeds. The advent of reliable clocks in cities and towns of the 1700s had a profound effect on the rhythms of everyday life. Instead of a day being defined by the rising and setting of the sun, clocks effectively regulated civic, commercial, and domestic life by breaking the day into smaller units of time to be managed.

In the coming years, inventors would expand and improve on wheel-based machines, creating ever-larger and more accurate devices. The wheel reached the pinnacle of its utility as the cornerstone of the world-changing Industrial Revolution.

THE FIRST ADDING MACHINE

Blaise Pascal is widely known today for his contributions to mathematics, probability theory, physics, and medicine. But during his lifetime, he was most known for his invention of the adding machine—the first digital calculator. As the story goes, at 19 years of age, Pascal made an adding machine to help his father with his tedious job as a tax collector in Rouen, France. The machine, which Pascal patented in 1649, had eight wheeled dials that could be set to a number from zero to nine. The wheels were linked together by a series of gears. When a number went from nine to zero, the number in the next column advanced. Pascal's invention worked similar to a car's odometer.

WHEEL-RELATED
INVENTIONS

GEARS

Clocks and many other mechanical devices would not operate without gears. Gears are wheels that interlock with each other using precisely spaced teeth, also called cogs. Gears transfer energy from one part of a machine to another. Gears are a way to increase speed or power, or they change the direction of power. The Greeks invented them in approximately 300 BCE.

Gears are critical components of many mechanical devices. When gears of different sizes are interlocked, the smaller gear turns faster to keep up with the rotation of the larger gear. The resulting speed creates power that leads to motion.

PULLEYS

Pulleys, also developed by the Greeks in approximately 300 BCE, are used for lifting or moving heavy objects. They multiply the force a person or a motor can exert. A one-wheel pulley with a rope looped over it allows a person to reverse the direction of the lifting force. For example, by applying 100 pounds (45 kg) of force, a person can raise a 100-pound box the same distance he or she pulls down on the rope. With a two-wheel pulley, that same person can lift the 100-pound box with only 50 pounds (23 kg) of force, though the box will only go one-half as far.[3] Greek mathematician Archimedes is credited with inventing the first compound pulley in approximately 220 BCE.

Pulleys operate according to the law of the conservation of energy, meaning the energy output must equal the energy input. Using a pulley to lift an object means a person can expend less energy, but must do so over a longer distance or time.

CRANKS

Cranks attach to an axle or shaft and are bent at a right angle. Turning a crank transfers circular motion into back-and-forth motion (called reciprocal motion). For example, turning a crank attached to a rod with a rope attached to it can raise a bucket from a well. Cranks did not come into wide use until the 1400s, when they were used to tighten crossbow strings and turn drills. Lynn White Jr., a medieval expert, noted, "Next to the wheel, the crank is the most important single mechanical device."[4]

Cranks magnify force because of leverage. There is an inverse relationship between speed and force: less force on the crank handle means proportionately more speed at the center of the crank, and more speed on the handle means less force at the center.

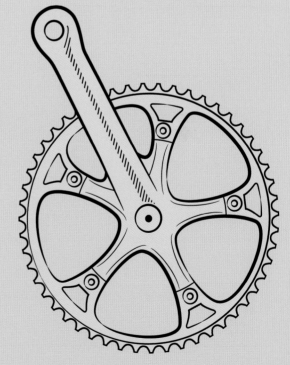

CHAPTER 5

REVOLUTION ON WHEELS

The Renaissance, lasting from approximately 1350 to 1700, was a time of learning, scientific discovery, world exploration, and colonization. It was also a time of invention, with people using the wheel in more creative ways to reduce labor and save time. With the help of wheeled inventions such as the steam engine and other forms of mechanization, the small local shops and mills of the Renaissance grew into the factories of the 1800s. The Industrial Revolution, encompassing the dramatic economic strides made from the mid-1700s through the 1800s, never could have occurred without the wheel.

The mechanization made possible by the wheel ignited the Industrial Revolution and led to massive economic and social changes during the 1800s.

WHEELED MUSICAL INSTRUMENTS

A number of musical instruments invented during the Renaissance and the Industrial Revolution use wheels. The hurdy-gurdy is a stringed instrument that sits on a player's lap. To produce a droning sound, the player turns a crank at the base of the instrument to rotate a wooden wheel. The wheel, much like the bow of a violin, rubs against two melody strings and four drone strings. Meanwhile, the player can alter the notes by pressing on any of the 24 keys. The glass harmonica, invented by Benjamin Franklin in 1761, consisted of 37 glass bowls mounted horizontally on an iron spindle and rotated with a foot treadle. Franklin designed the instrument after watching a performer rub the rims of water goblets to produce sound. The player piano, introduced in the late 1800s, produces its musical magic through a roll of paper that attaches to a rotating spool. As the spool turns, air blows over holes in the paper, causing valves in the piano's hammers to rise and fall in the proper sequence.

The changes brought by the wheeled machines of the Industrial Revolution were revolutionary. The craftsmen of earlier eras became the factory laborers of the 1800s; they owned no tools of their own and had limited skills. Economic power switched from many small family enterprises to big industries owned by only a few people. Laborers organized into labor unions to gain more power, and working people who were frustrated with rising social inequality were drawn to political movements that promoted the sharing of wealth, such as communism, by the 1900s. But even with the well-chronicled hardships of the times, wheeled machinery made life better in countless ways. Mass-produced goods cost less than handcrafted goods. And laborsaving devices increased leisure time, allowing more people to become educated and join the growing middle class as doctors, engineers, academics, attorneys, and managers. There was also more time to pursue the arts and other creative endeavors. Wheeled machines even helped women gain more independence.

Spinning Jenny and Spinning Mule

In the 1700s, mass-produced yarn became possible with the combination of two wheel-based inventions—the waterwheel and the spinning wheel. First, in 1764, English mechanic James Hargreaves invented the spinning jenny. It consisted of a spinning frame powered by a hand crank, and it allowed one operator to make eight strands of cotton yarn at the same time. A few years later, Samuel Crompton, an English weaver, created the spinning mule. The spinning mule, powered by a waterwheel, could produce 48 strands of fine, high-quality yarn at once.[1] The spinning mule met the increasing demand for clothing and household goods for a growing European population.

Steam Engines

Waterwheels and windmills did a fine job grinding flour and spinning thread. But when the wind did not blow or a lack of rain caused

Fearing the spinning jenny would take their jobs, textile workers broke into James Hargreaves's home and destroyed his machines.

rivers to flow too slowly, power failed and industry came to a stop. Steam engines were invented in response to the increasing demand for an unending power supply for mining, transportation, and manufacturing.

A steam engine uses burning coal or wood to heat water in a large boiler. The pressurized steam is captured and directed to a round metal tube in which a piston slides back and forth. The expanding steam moves the piston, which then turns a crank to create motion. In the case of a steam locomotive, a crank converts the back-and-forth energy of the piston into the circular energy required to turn the locomotive's wheels. The first practical steam engine was invented in 1698 by Englishman Thomas Savery, refined by Englishman Thomas Newcomen in 1712, and perfected by Scotsman James Watt in 1765.

In addition to providing reliable power, steam engines did not have to be located near moving water or wind. As long as a steam engine had a supply of coal and some stored water, it could keep running. By the time the Industrial Revolution took hold, steam engines were powering textile mills and pumping water out of mines. Steam engines were also powering vehicles, including farm tractors, cable cars, railroad locomotives, and steamboats. The age of steam power changed Europe, North America, and eventually the world. Steam-powered machines fostered the expansion of factories and industry

Today, steam continues to provide much of the world's power. The steam from burning coal or gas spins the blades of huge steam turbines, which provide the power for many electric generators.

like never before. Steam-powered vehicles moved more goods and people than could have been imagined only decades prior.

Flywheels

Though steam power was not as intermittent as wind and waterpower, early steam engines had one cylinder that transferred energy only on its forward stroke, providing a less-than-ideal source of power for machines that worked better with smooth, continuous power. Flywheels solved this problem by acting as a kind of spinning mechanical battery that stored enough energy to keep the engine turning between power strokes. Flywheels, which are often made of metal and have a heavy rim, transform bursts of energy into smooth movement.

The steam engine gets the flywheel started, and then the flywheel continues spinning, providing a continuous source of energy until it slows down and the steam

Since steam engines were too expensive for most farmers to buy on their own, some pooled their money to hire a traveling steam-powered thresher.

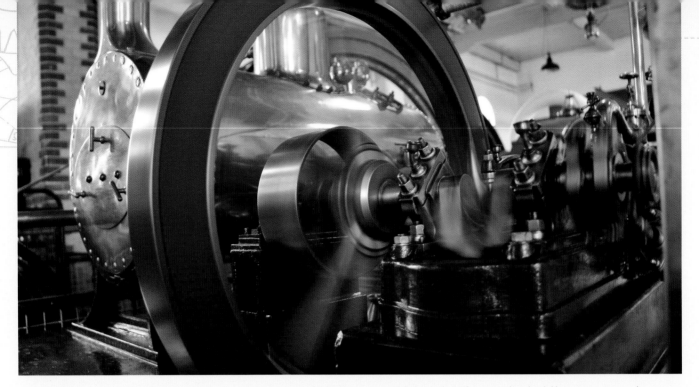

Flywheels are wheels that provide temporary storage of kinetic energy. It takes a lot of energy to start them spinning and a lot of energy to stop them. The faster the speed, the more kinetic energy is stored.

engine sends it spinning again. Human-powered flywheels were used in ancient times, such as the kick wheels that turned potter's wheels. Flywheels found a modern home in the Industrial Revolution.

Wheeled Machines and the Emancipation of Women

In the Industrial Revolution, a pair of wheeled machines—the sewing machine and the typewriter—opened new employment opportunities for women. After several inventors struggled to come up with a successful sewing machine,

BALL BEARINGS AND DRIVE CHAIN

Two Industrial Revolution—era inventions made wheeled machines and vehicles operate more efficiently, the ball bearing and the drive chain. Ball bearings greatly improved wheels by reducing friction. The principle behind their effectiveness is that there is less friction when moving parts roll past each other than when they slide, particularly when they are lubricated with oil. The ball bearings used in modern machinery were developed by Philip Vaughan in 1794 to support an axle on a carriage. The first drive chain, invented in 1864 by James Slater in Britain for use on a bicycle, employed a chain with rollers that fit precisely over the cogs of a sprocket. The drive chain effectively enabled several transfers of energy to produce motion, because pedaling advanced the drive chain over the cogs and turned the sprocket, which in turn caused the wheels to rotate.

American machinist Elias Howe demonstrated a machine in 1845 that he said took the place of five seamstresses. The machine included a number of wheels, gears, and spindles to send a needle and thread through two layers of cloth. After not achieving commercial success for his invention in either Great Britain or the United States, Howe decided to license his machine to competing inventor Isaac Singer. The sewing machine revolutionized the garment-making industry and greatly expanded opportunities for women to work outside their homes.

In 1868, American newspaper editor Christopher Latham Sholes patented the first typewriter, a device with keys that printed letters onto paper, which then advanced on a wheeled roll. The typewriter caught on in the 1870s and 1880s, opening up a new class of jobs for women. Before then, almost all secretaries were male apprentices with aspirations of moving up in their companies. Young women of this era gravitated to office jobs, as working in a factory,

Young women from rural areas flocked to cities to work in the garment industry. Many immigrants also found work in garment factories, which often had terrible working conditions.

being a seamstress, or providing household help were looked down upon as lower-class employment. Employers were happy to hire women as stenographers and typewriter operators instead of men, as they typically paid women half as much. By 1890, nearly 1,300 training schools operated throughout the United States to teach typewriting and stenographic skills to an eager pool of learners, and by 1910, 81 percent of typists were female.[2]

Wheeled Machines of War

The 1800s saw a number of military-related wheeled inventions. In England in the 1820s, an inventor created a wheel-like revolving cylinder with chambers to hold bullets that would align with the barrel for firing—the revolver. An American, Samuel Colt, made the first reliable revolver, and the first mass-produced revolvers were made in 1857 by the Smith and Wesson Company. In 1862, American Richard Jordan Gatling patented a hand-cranked rifle with ten barrels, which rotated and rapidly fired more than 300 rounds per minute—the first machine gun.[3]

Wheels also played a role in improving military transportation. In 1846, James Boydell, managing partner of an English ironworking company, patented a wheel that was designed to prevent vehicles from sinking into loose dirt and mud. Boydell figured out a way to attach pivoting boards around the circumference of the wheel. As the wheel rolled forward, two sections of the boards would lay flat on the ground to distribute the wheel's load over a broader area. The invention, which is viewed as the precursor of continuous-track locomotion as used in tanks and construction equipment today, was put to use by the British army in 1856 during the Crimean War.

CHAPTER 6

WHEELED VEHICLES
SPEED UP

Americans or Europeans born in 1810 would have found their world unrecognizable by their eightieth birthday. Due to changes made possible by wheeled machines, towns grew into cities, and high-rise buildings sent cities reaching for the sky. More amazing wheeled inventions were still to come. For thousands of years, the cart's basic wheel and axle design changed little. Although wheeled vehicles varied greatly in exterior style and function—from two-wheeled English gigs and French chaises to American stagecoaches and Conestoga wagons—they all employed wooden-spoke wheels with sectioned wooden rims and wood or iron tires. That changed in the Industrial Revolution when the

Steam locomotives opened up the western United States to expansion, particularly after the completion of the transcontinental railroad in 1869.

wheeled vehicles people today take for granted—such as the train, bicycle, and automobile—forever changed the social and economic landscape. Travel became faster, cheaper, more comfortable, and available to greater numbers of people.

Railroad

As essential as steam engines were to manufacturing during the Industrial Revolution, they were just as important to wheeled transportation—particularly the steam locomotive. English engineer Richard Trevithick built the first successful steam locomotive in 1803. Once the steam locomotive was introduced, railroads expanded rapidly. In 1830, there were only 95 miles (153 km) of track in England. By 1890, England had 20,000 miles (32,200 km) of track, and the expanding United States had a railroad network spanning more than 167,000 miles (268,700 km).[1]

The economic and political effects of railroads were enormous. Hauling time decreased, lowering freight costs. In the United States, the railroad opened up more land for farming, particularly in the interior of the country, because farmers could more easily and cheaply get their crops to market. However, more crops caused prices to drop and put some farmers out of business. Railroad magnates acquired enormous political power and reaped huge financial rewards, as they held a near monopoly on the most efficient means of transporting goods. Rumbling social unrest caused the US government to begin regulating railroad rates and other private enterprises to avoid the social revolutions taking place among working-class people in Europe.

On the whole, though, access to commercial and passenger rail service was a huge benefit. With the completion of the transcontinental railway in the United States, a journey across the country was cut from a difficult several months to an easy six or seven days. When famine or other disasters struck, emergency responders could quickly send food, medical supplies, or people to help. Products became more readily available, and consumers could purchase them for less money because transportation was quicker and cheaper.

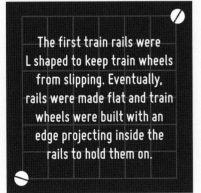
STOCKTON AND DARLINGTON RAILWAY

On September 27, 1825, the world's first steam railroad opened. The owner of an English coal mine had originally planned on using horse-drawn carts to haul ore from a mine in Darlington, England, to the seaport of Stockton, England. But engineer George Stephenson convinced the owner that a steam engine could pull 50 times more weight than a horse.[2] The Stockton & Darlington railway inspired the use of railroads throughout the world.

Bicycle

German Baron von Drais invented the first bicycle in 1817, and many other inventors improved upon it, including Englishman James Starley. Starley's tangent-spoke bicycle was a resounding success, but there were problems with his towering Ariel model. The high seats made mounting and dismounting the bike difficult. Falls were frequent and dangerous.

Although some "safety" bicycles were introduced in the late 1800s, none caught on. John Kemp Starley, James Starley's nephew, wondered if he could succeed where others had failed. In 1885, four years after his uncle's death, he introduced the Rover, a low-mount bicycle with wheels of equal size. It was the first modern bicycle, and its basic design continues to this day.

The Rover proved popular with riders of all kinds, particularly women. In fact, similar to the sewing machine and typewriter, the bicycle is given significant credit for the emancipation of middle- and upper-class women. During the bicycling craze of the late 1800s, women were liberated from the hoop skirts and corsets of the Victorian era. Fueled by the call for more practical clothing by Amelia Jenks Bloomer, a women's rights campaigner, women took to their bikes in cycling knickerbockers—widely referred to as bloomers.

The bicycle also fostered much-needed road improvements. After railroads decreased the demand for horse-drawn coaches, more and more

The revolutionary design of the Rover bicycle won the favor of riders because of its decided safety advantages over high wheelers.

people took to the roads on bikes. Bicycling enthusiasts in Western Europe and the United States demanded better road surfaces and signage, so in more ways than one, these riders paved the way for the automobiles yet to come.

Automobile

The search for a useful motorized road vehicle required a long period of trial and error. The earliest autos were powered by steam engines, the only means of power at the time. French military engineer Nicolas-Joseph Cugnot is given credit for the first successful automobile, a steam-powered gun carriage he built in 1769. Cugnot's second vehicle, built the following year, chugged along at a walking speed of three miles per hour (5 kmh) and has the distinction of being involved in the first automobile crash when it ran into a wall![3]

German engineers Karl Benz and Gottlieb Daimler recognized the potential of the gasoline engine for powering road vehicles. Benz built his first three-wheeled car in 1885, and in 1886 Daimler built a four-wheeled car. Brothers Frank and Charles Duryea built the first gasoline-powered car in the United States in 1893. In 1908, Henry Ford made

THE END OF CONVERSATION

A columnist for the *London Spectator* was of the opinion that the bicycle would ruin enlightened conversation. In 1896, he wrote, "If people can pedal away ten miles [16 km] or so in the middle of the day to a lunch for which they need no dress, where the talk is haphazard, varied, light, and only too easy; and then glide back in the cool of the afternoon to dine quietly and get early to bed . . . conversation of the more serious type will tend to go out."[4]

automobiles affordable for the average family with the mass-produced Model T. Within several decades, the mobility made possible by gasoline-powered vehicles was influencing everything from interstate commerce to social customs to the growth of suburbia.

Paddle-Wheel Steamboat

By 500 CE, the Chinese had developed a man-powered paddle-wheel boat, but the full development of the paddle wheel had to wait for the steam engine in the 1800s. In the same way the steam locomotive revolutionized overland transportation, the steam engine transformed water transportation. It allowed goods to be shipped faster, farther, and more cheaply than had been possible with wind- or man-powered boats.

American Robert Fulton built the first practical steamship in 1807. An onboard steam engine powered a large paddle wheel situated at the rear or side of the vessel. Paddle-wheel steamboats soon took over river transportation throughout the world. Seafarers tried oceangoing paddle wheels, but the paddles tended to lift out of the water in rough seas. Also, in the

The Benz Motorwagen was the first motor vehicle sold to the public. It had a top speed of nine miles per hour (14 kmh), similar to the trotting speed of a horse.

ROADS REPAIRED

With the fall of the Roman Empire, roads fell into disrepair and few new ones were constructed. It was not until the 1600s, when France began using forced labor for building and maintaining roads, that the number and quality of roads increased. At the same time in England, toll roads came into existence, and enough fees were collected to build more than 20,000 miles (32,000 km) of turnpikes by the 1830s.[6] With the invention of bicycles, asphalt for paving, and automobiles, road building in the late 1800s and early 1900s finally returned to its former Roman glory.

case of naval ships, the paddle wheels were fully exposed and subject to attack. Screw propellers, which are spinning discs with blades attached at a central hub, offered the advantage of taking up less room and being less vulnerable to attack because they operated underwater. After the British navy conducted a series of head-to-head races in 1845 between a propeller-driven ship and one powered by a paddle wheel, all new steam-powered ships they built were propeller driven.

Both sail and steam powered the CSS *Nashville*. As a Confederate ship, the *Nashville* successfully passed through the Union blockade of Beaufort, South Carolina, during the American Civil War (1861–1865) to deliver cargo and necessary provisions.

Farm Vehicles

In combination with the railroad, new wheeled farm machinery—including the tractor, reaper, and cotton gin—revolutionized farming. These laborsaving devices allowed more land to be farmed, and they accelerated the change from family farming to large-scale industrial farming. Enterprising farmers and corporations capitalized on the opportunity to farm large sections of land. The availability of rail transportation meant their products could be sold even to distant consumers. British inventor Richard Edgeworth patented a vehicle with a rolling "portable railway" in

1770, but it was not until American Benjamin Holt invented his steam-powered, crawler-type tractor in 1904 that use of this technology took off.

The cotton gin, invented by another American, Eli Whitney, in 1793, revolutionized cotton production in the United States. When pulled by a mule, the gin allowed a single worker to process as much raw cotton as 50 workers—and with much less effort.[7]

While demonstrating his newly invented horse-drawn reaper in 1831, Cyrus McCormick cut six acres (2.4 ha) of oats in one day, doing the work of six men. Below the machine's axle, steel fingers separated grain stalks into bunches, and a saw-tooth cutting bar slid sideways and cut the stalks. Power for the cutting blade came from one of the wheels.

The wheel revolutionized transportation in the Industrial Revolution, but its full effect would not be felt until the modern era, when the growth of technology accelerated beyond anyone's imagination.

Eli Whitney's cotton gin worked like a sieve. A row of hooks pulled raw cotton through a wooden drum and a mesh filter, but the seeds were left behind.

THE RUBBER TIRE

Carts and wagons changed dramatically with time, but their wheels and tires changed little. Tires—thin strips of wood or metal that were lashed, riveted, or molded to the wooden wheel rim—did little to soften the wheels' bumpy and uncomfortable ride. That changed with the discovery of rubber and the invention of the rubber tire.

Since the 1700s, European explorers had been bringing home a milky sap from South American trees that could erase pencil marks and be molded into bouncing balls. Named rubber, the substance first found its way into shoes and waterproof coats, but it melted in the summer and stiffened in the winter. In 1839, American Charles Goodyear found a way to vulcanize, or harden, rubber by adding sulfur.

In 1845, Scottish engineer Robert Thomson filled rubber tubes with air—the first pneumatic tires—and attached them to the wheels of a carriage. But the pneumatic tire did not catch on until Scottish inventor John Dunlop installed them on bicycles in 1887 and they became popular with cyclists. Dunlop's tire consisted of an inner rubber tube containing compressed air and an outer rubber casing that provided road traction and protection from puncture. These tires were quickly adapted to the automobile, and today both natural and synthetic rubber is used to manufacture tires.

After years of experimenting, being jailed for debt, and being scorned by fellow scientists, Charles Goodyear finally learned how to stabilize rubber at all temperatures.

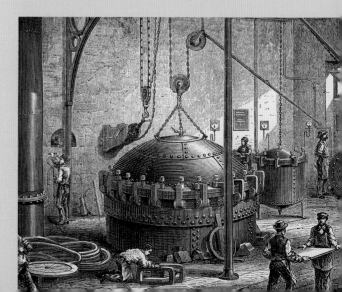

The advent of synthetic rubber in the 1930s made it possible for tire production to expand to meet the rising demand for motor vehicles. Today, tires of every size, shape, and tread carry vehicles over the roads.

Passenger car tires are made up of the tread, the sidewall, and the bead. The tread is the patterned part of the rubber that comes in contact with the road. The sidewall gives shape to the tire and supports the tread. The bead is a rubber-covered bundle of wires on the edge of the tire that connects the tire to the wheel. The tire's physical design and the chemistry of its raw materials make it suitable for various conditions, such as cold, snow, rain, or heat. The tire-to-rim connection has improved over time so inner tubes are no longer needed in automobile tires.

Today, tires can be found not only on bicycles and automobiles, but also on trucks, buses, airplanes, tractors, forklifts, baby strollers, wheelchairs, and motorcycles. Tire manufacturers make approximately 1 billion tires a year.[8] Manufacturers of automobile tires now routinely offer 80,000-mile (128,748 km) warranties on their products.[9] Engineers are working on non-pneumatic tires that will never go flat owing to their unique, load-bearing spoke structure in place of air.

CHAPTER 7

MODERN
WHEELS

T he age of electricity made many wheeled machines of the past obsolete. For example, the spinning wheel was replaced by the steam-operated spinning jenny, which in turn was replaced by electrically operated textile mills. But with electricity came a flood of new wheel-based inventions. And it was perhaps wheeled vehicles that saw the most dramatic changes in the 1900s and had the greatest effect on society.

Wheeled Machines in the 1900s

Many wheel-using machines of the 1900s made life easier and more comfortable. Devices and machines including the can opener, rotary

Widespread use of the automobile changed how we travel and how we plan our cities.

ROLLER SKATES

In the 1800s, people began to take wheeled fun seriously. M. Petitbled of France patented the first roller skate in 1819, fashioning it after ice skates with a single row of wheels. The four-wheeled skate, invented by American James Plimpton in 1863, rolled more easily and gave the skater more control. This "quad" skate became the standard throughout most of the 1900s. Skate innovations included the adjustable clamp-on skate in 1905 and a return to inline skating with the advent of the Rollerblade in 1986. Roller skating still offers serious fun for many. Rink hockey, inline hockey, and roller figure skating are also popular. Roller Derby, a team sport involving vigorous body contact as competitors race around the rink, is one of the fastest-growing sports, with more than 1,500 leagues in 40 countries.[1]

telephone, electric fan, and air conditioner, to name a few, changed how people lived and communicated. Office equipment, such as the ballpoint pen (with its ball-bearing tip), electric typewriter, and drum copy machine, simplified office tasks. Of course, no wheel-using machine would change office and home life quite like the computer has.

The jet engine made it possible for manufacturers to build larger aircraft that could fly longer and faster than propeller airplanes, thus making air travel more appealing and attainable for the masses. Motion pictures, record players, and videocassette recorders provided entertainment, while wheeled sports such as roller skating and skateboarding offered new ways to exercise and have fun.

Computer

Today's computer components are mostly digital, meaning there are no moving parts. But wheels have played an important role in storing and retrieving data. In 1956, IBM introduced the IBM 350 RAMAC (Random

IBM's RAMAC 350 was the first computer hard drive, and its 50 spinning disks had a capacity of 5 million characters. The unit was 60 inches (152 cm) wide, 68 inches (173 cm) tall, 29 inches (74 cm) deep, and it weighed 600 pounds (270 kg).

Access Method of Accounting and Control). This early mainframe computer consisted of a stack of 50 magnetic disk drives, each two feet (0.6 m) in diameter, all rotating at 1,200 revolutions per minute.[2]

As computers evolved, both large mainframes and newer personal computers continued using rotating magnetic disk drives, called hard drives, to store information on close concentric tracks—up to 20,000 tracks per inch (8,000 tracks per cm).[3] Today's disks rotate at up to 15,000 revolutions per minute.[4] Magnetic tape and optical discs (CD-ROMs) are also used for computer data storage.

Jet Engine

The first practical demonstration of a flying machine was in 1903 when American brothers Orville and Wilbur Wright flew their gas-powered, aluminum-engine airplane at Kitty Hawk, North Carolina. Once propeller-driven planes became streamlined with an enclosed cabin and retractable wheels, the only thing limiting airspeed was a faster engine. Beginning in 1928, Englishman Frank Whittle worked on his idea to combine a rocket engine with a gas turbine, obtaining a patent for his turbojet engine in 1930. At the same time in Germany, Hans von Ohain was working on a similar concept.

The jet engine, also called a turbojet or gas turbine, differs from a rocket engine in that it requires oxygen from the atmosphere for combustion. In contrast, rocket engines are self-contained and carry all the fuel components they need, thus making them more suitable for space travel outside the atmosphere. The key component of a jet engine is a large fan, which works similar to a wheel. The fan sucks air into a compressor made up of more twirling fans, raising the

FANS POWER JET ENGINES

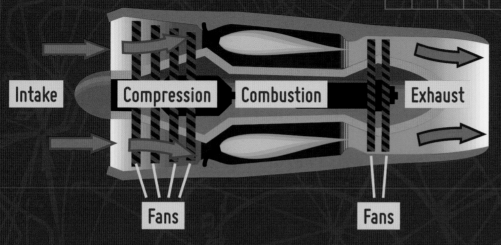

Intake • Compression • Combustion • Exhaust

Fans

Fans

Without either spinning propellers or the powerful fans of a jet engine (shown here by striped bars), both based on the wheel, airplanes would never have enough power or lift to leave the ground.

air pressure. The compressed air is squeezed into a combustion chamber, where it is sprayed with fuel and ignited with an electric spark. The burning gas expands, rotates turbine blades, and blasts out the back of the engine, thrusting the engine, and its attached aircraft, forward.

The British Overseas Airways Corporation offered the first commercial flight using jet engines in 1952. This London-to-Johannesburg service was discontinued a few years later, as metal fatigue from extreme changes in temperature and air pressure resulted in several crashes. It was not until the advent of the American Boeing 707 in 1959 that long-distance commercial air travel became widely available. The power and capacity of the engine made

WHEELED VEHICLES IN OUTER SPACE

Rocket engines made it possible for wheeled vehicles to find their way into outer space. On three American missions to the moon—Apollo 15 in 1971, Apollo 16 in 1972, and Apollo 17 in 1972—astronauts used lunar rovers to explore the moon's surface. The Soviet Union landed two Lunokhod wheeled robotic vehicles on the moon in 1970 and 1973. In 1997, NASA landed the Sojourner craft on Mars. As of 2014, Mars Spirit and Opportunity (both of which landed in 2004), and Mars Curiosity (which landed in 2012), have traveled a combined 35 miles (56 km) across the red planet while conducting scientific experiments.[8]

the world a much smaller place. It took Christopher Columbus two months to sail from Spain to the Bahamas in 1492.[5] Today, a voyage on the Queen Mary II from England to New York takes seven days.[6] A flight from London to New York in a commercial jet airliner takes close to seven hours.[7]

Wheels in Entertainment

Movies, phonograph records, videotapes, and DVDs have all fueled modern culture. During World War II (1939–1945), movie theaters in the United States showed short films prior to the feature presentation to encourage support for the war effort. Newspapers printed on giant, spinning rolls of paper shared news of the day from around the world. News and opinion in the mid-1900s could be heard, seen, and read by millions of people instead of only the people in the village square.

A number of people have been credited with inventing motion pictures, including Thomas Edison and Louis Jean Lumière of France in the late 1800s. Using perforated strips of film that wind around a wheeled drum, the shutters of modern motion picture cameras open 24 times every second, exposing the film and advancing the reel. In recent years, many filmmakers have shifted to digital technology owing to ease of editing and distribution, though some still prefer the artistic effects available through film.

Thomas Edison, a prolific inventor, also patented the first phonograph in 1878. In his earliest version, a stylus that responded to sound vibrations carved lines into tinfoil wrapped around a spinning cylinder. A different stylus then passed over the same grooves to replay the recorded sound, or at least a crude version of it. The means of preserving recorded sound evolved with time, from Edison's tinfoil to a wax cylinder and then to horizontal discs made of various materials. By the early 1900s, millions of phonograph records were being made. These early records featured only four or five minutes of audio recording each, so Peter Goldmark of Columbia Broadcasting System (CBS) began experimenting after World War II with recording sound onto vinyl discs using very narrow grooves. The first long-playing records (LPs) came on the market in 1948, allowing more than 20 minutes of playing time per side.[9]

Major movies shot on 35 mm film are often scanned into a digital format so they can be inexpensively duplicated and shown on digital projectors. By 2013, only one-third of movie theaters worldwide still used 35mm projectors.[10]

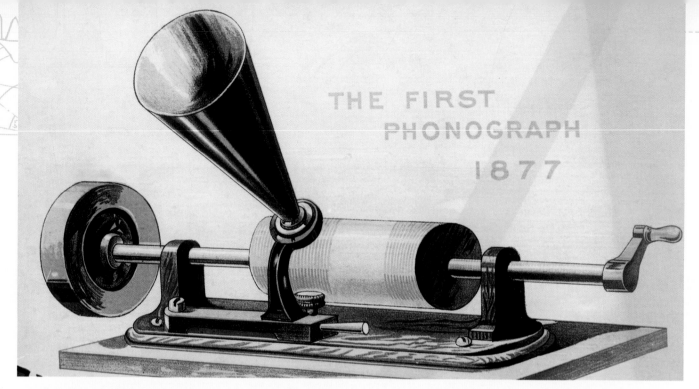

THE FIRST PHONOGRAPH 1877

While Thomas Edison was seeking a way to improve the telegraph transmitter, he discovered that running the paper tape through the machine at a high speed produced sound resembling spoken words. The first words Edison successfully recorded on his phonograph with a tinfoil cylinder were "Mary Had a Little Lamb."

A videotape recorder converts visual information into electrical impulses and saves the digital information onto magnetic tape. The tape wraps from one wheel to another, with the recording or playback device positioned between the two reels. The videotape recorder was first developed in 1951 by American engineer John Mullin and enhanced by Japanese corporations through their development of videocassettes in both the VHS and Betamax formats.

Videocassette recorders (VCRs) ushered in a new era in home entertainment, as consumers could watch television programs and movies at their leisure.

The digital video disc (DVD) was patented by David Paul Gregg in 1958 and first used by MCA Entertainment Company in 1978. Lasers etch digital patterns to represent pictures and audio onto the reflective surface of the DVD, and then the DVD player plays back the information when a light beam reads the DVD surface.

Wheeled Vehicles in the 1900s

Perhaps nothing in the 1900s changed more rapidly than the wheeled vehicle, and it seems likely that nothing had more of an effect on daily life. For better or for worse, by the 1930s, cars and trucks were in widespread use and changed the American landscape—from the massive construction of highways and interstate freeways to the advent of motels and drive-in theaters.

HELICOPTER

Helicopters are wheeled vehicles even though they have no wheels making contact with the ground. A helicopter's rotor acts like a windmill in reverse—instead of wind blowing blades and turning a shaft, the helicopter's motor rotates angled blades, which move air and cause lift. Designs for helicopters go back centuries. Ancient Chinese toys used a pull string to launch a spindle with wooden blades into the air. Leonardo da Vinci sketched an aerial-screw machine in 1483. It took a long time to put the dream into practice. Experimental helicopters, or autogyros as they were called, did not find success until 1939 when a test model built by Igor Sikorsky became the prototype for future helicopters. The US Army improved on Sikorsky's design and had 400 helicopters in the air by the end of World War II.[13] Because the helicopter can land vertically practically anywhere—from rooftops to mountaintops—it has played an important role in military, urban, and rough-terrain rescues.

To be sure, the domination of the automobile came as a mixed blessing. Although cars made transportation easier and allowed roads to be free of horse manure, they also filled the air with exhaust and clogged the streets with traffic. Cars gave people freedom, autonomy, and better access to goods and medical care, but by 1980, vehicle accidents killed nearly 50,000 Americans every year.[11] In 1982, the automobile industry provided one of every six American jobs.[12] But a few short years later, many autoworkers lost their jobs when factories moved overseas and/or tasks were taken over by robots.

The availability of trucks, jeeps, tanks, and other military vehicles changed the nature of warfare during the numerous conflicts of the 1900s. In contrast to previous centuries, soldiers in the 1900s, along with their weapons, could be transported quickly and in mass numbers by truck, train, or air. Tanks, now a mainstay of ground warfare, made their first appearance in World War I (1914–1918) when British troops needed a way to cross the enemy's rugged terrain, barbed wire barriers, and deep trenches. Although design flaws and mechanical difficulties plagued these early tanks, they were an asset in some battles and became a standard component of military arsenals.

Wheels and Tires

Improvements to the internal combustion engine brought greater speed, more power, and better fuel efficiency to the automobile. New wheel designs contributed to these improvements, too. In the early 1920s, many car manufacturers began replacing the spoke wheel of the Model T with disc wheels. Ironically, the one-piece disc resembled the solid wooden wheel that came into existence 6,000 years before. Stamped out of sheet metal, the metal disc was sturdy and relatively light, and it was easily mass produced and inexpensive. The wheel's unattractive appearance was remedied with decorative wheel covers. By adding chrome wheel covers and wide, whitewall tires, wheels became as stylish as the cars they carried. Spoke wheels began making a comeback after aluminum-cast auto parts were introduced in the 1960s. Using aluminum and magnesium made wheels even lighter and stronger.

Tires also went through dramatic changes in the later 1900s. The narrow rubber tire widened and was updated with new materials. The radial tire, introduced by the tire manufacturer Michelin in the 1950s, consisted of crisscrossed fabric and belts of steel, polyester, and other sturdy fibers. Specialized treads were molded into the outer surface to work well under specific road conditions. A vehicle's wheels are so integral to people's driving experiences that the word *wheels* became synonymous with *vehicle*.

Wheels for Work and Play

The 1900s saw a great leap in the variety of wheeled vehicles available. By the 1950s to the 1980s, consumers could buy a station wagon, van, or sport-utility vehicle to carry their family. Urban dwellers and ranchers alike could select from large and small pickup trucks. Huge semi-trucks with 18 wheels carried food and goods across the country. Vehicles also shrank to two-seater sports cars, gas-conserving compact cars, and the two-wheeled Segway that carried a single person standing upright.

The economic gains fostered by the Industrial Revolution made it possible for consumers in the early 1900s to enjoy more disposable income, as well as more leisure time. By the 1920s, as cars became more affordable and highways were built, trailer parks and campgrounds sprang up around national parks and other attractions. Although most people used tents for their outdoor stays, demand grew for a more convenient form of camping. By the mid-1930s, close to 400 different companies, including Airstream, were building travel trailers.[14] Today they are

SKATEBOARD

Skateboards began appearing in the 1950s in California, but no one knows who invented the first one. Most likely surfers waiting for some good waves created this form of wheeled recreation. The earliest skateboards were made by screwing roller skate wheels onto a wooden board or box. The first metal-wheeled skateboards were mass-produced in 1959, and then clay wheels took over in the early 1960s. The musical group Jan and Dean sang "Sidewalk Surfing" in 1964, and skateboarding never looked back. The introduction of urethane wheels in 1973 made boards smoother, quieter, and better at gripping concrete, banks, and ditches. In recent years, elaborate skate parks have opened in thousands of communities throughout the United States, surging from only three in the whole nation in 1996 to more than 350 in California alone by 2011.[15] Skateboarding has provided kids with transportation, independence, sport, and injuries for several generations.

called recreational vehicles, or RVs, and can include tent trailers, truck campers, sport-utility trailers, travel trailers, and motor homes.

Not to be confused with the RV, the ATV (all-terrain vehicle) includes three- and four-wheeled vehicles designed for off-road use. In 1967, Honda Motorcycles wanted a product its dealers could sell in the winter when motorcycle sales dropped off. The result was the 1969 Honda US90, which was basically a motorcycle with three large wheels that could be driven in snow, mud, and sand. Other Japanese motorcycle manufacturers followed suit, with Yamaha, Kawasaki, and Suzuki coming out with ATVs of their own. Not solely a recreational vehicle, the ATV is also used as a working vehicle where navigable roads do not exist.

In the second half of the 1900s, wheels played an integral part in the rise of the second-most watched sport in America: automobile racing. NASCAR, which sponsors multiple auto racing events, trails only professional football in television viewership. From the leading corporations that invest heavily in sponsoring racing teams to the legion of passionate fans who cheer for their favorite drivers, NASCAR is a huge and growing enterprise in the sports world. Drivers employ cutting-edge automotive technology on everything from fuel-injected engines to tire inflation to increase their speed and gain an advantage over competitors.

Although the wheel enabled great technological advances in countless areas of life during the 1900s, it also contributed negative effects such as environmental degradation. With the smog created by motor vehicles and the pollution caused by myriad industries that used wheel-based technology, the wheel created new problems while solving others. In any event, there was no turning back to life before the wheel; on the contrary, wheeled inventions would continue to zoom into the next century.

ATVs are popular recreational vehicles, but their capacity for speed and their high center of gravity lead to many accidents.

CHAPTER 8

THE WHEEL
ROLLS ON

T he wheels that rotate inside today's complex machines and
carry modern vehicles could not be more different from
the first potter's wheels and wooden carts. Yet they all use
the same science—flat discs rotating on axles. Inside inventors'
minds, the simple wheel has always held limitless possibilities
and applications. Today and into the future, creative people will
continue to find new and unique ways to put the wheel to work.
And the devices they create may continue to fuel controversy and
change society.

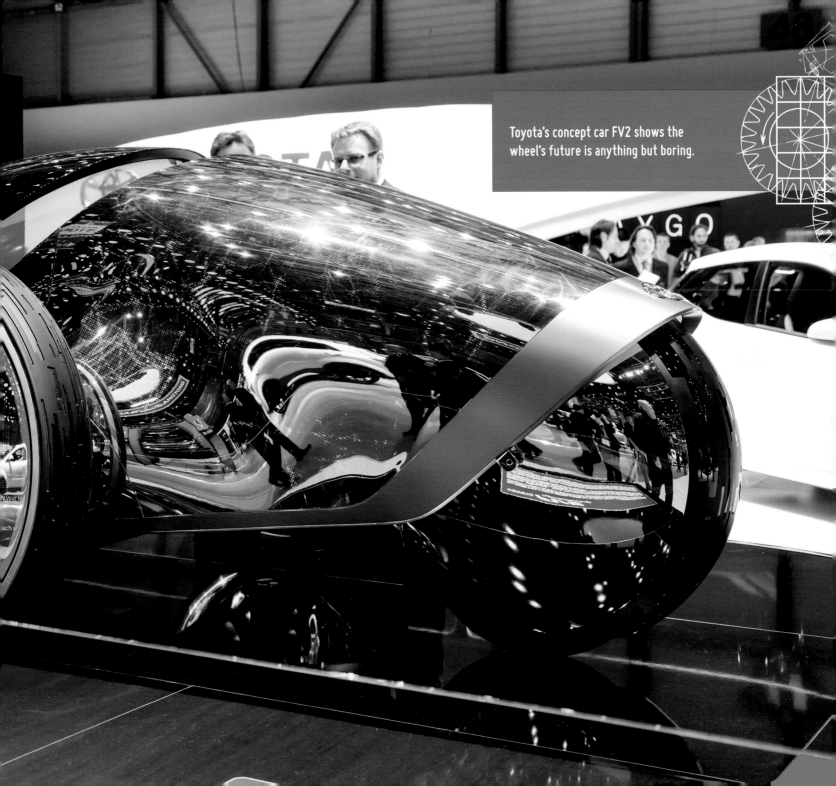

Toyota's concept car FV2 shows the wheel's future is anything but boring.

NO MORE STEERING WHEEL

The UC? electric car, built by Rinspeed of Switzerland in 2010, lacks some of the basic equipment found in other cars: a steering wheel and foot pedals! Instead, the UC?, which stands for "urban commuter," is operated with a joy stick much like those used for video games. The two-seat, all-electric car is equipped to be easily loaded onto a train, so drivers have the option of combining several means of transportation in one trip. Similar to many of the innovative cars designed by Rinspeed's founder, automotive visionary Frank Rinderknecht, there are no plans to put the UC? into commercial production.

The Tweel

Although the pneumatic tire was a great advance for road and off-road travel 100 years ago, it has always had one large drawback: it can be punctured and go flat. In 2005, the Michelin tire company introduced an improvement to the pneumatic tire—the Tweel airless tire. The Tweel, whose name is a combination of *tire* and *wheel*, is made up of a rigid hub, flexible spokes, a steel-belted inner band, and an outer tread. Strong spokes and the tension of the steel-belted band replace the air pressure that holds up a traditional tire.

When the Tweel runs over an object, the tread, band, and spokes deform to absorb the impact and then spring back to their original shape. In their current design, Tweels vibrate when driven more than 50 miles per hour (80 kmh), leading to loud noise

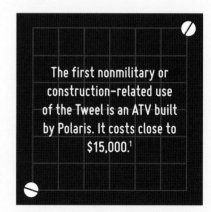

The first nonmilitary or construction-related use of the Tweel is an ATV built by Polaris. It costs close to $15,000.[1]

and excessive heat production.[2] Because of these drawbacks, Tweels are only used at low speeds such as on construction and military vehicles.

Active Wheel System

The Active Wheel System (AWS), first developed by the Michelin tire company in 1996, could be the most advanced design in the evolution of the wheel. In an AWS, the components that make a car run—the motor, suspension, gearbox, and transmission— are all housed within the wheel itself. Because the drive motor is electric, the AWS can only be used in hybrid (gas/electric), plug-in, or battery-run vehicles, rather than cars with only internal combustion engines. When AWS technology is used on all four wheels, there are no axles, as each wheel operates

Michelin's non-pneumatic Tweel is available in a smooth tread for hard surfaces, as well as two kinds of grooved treads for use on turf and rugged terrain.

independently from the others. Cars with AWS enable superior road handling, because each AWS wheel is able to respond to the specific road conditions it encounters.

Without an engine or axles taking up space, the AWS could foster dramatic changes in car design. Smaller cars would have room to carry more people or cargo, and larger, stronger impact-absorbing zones could be added to the front and rear ends of the cars. The first AWS cars were scheduled to go on the market in 2010, but as of 2015, it was not known when this new wheel technology would be available to consumers.

Wheeled Space Station

The invention of the wheel helped mankind survive more comfortably on Earth. In space, the wheel may be necessary for humankind to survive at all. The International Space Station (ISS) is a marvel of technology, but the teams of astronauts who return from the station experience a loss

THE WHEEL'S REPLACEMENT?

According to inventors James Powell and Gordon Danby, magnetic levitation (Maglev) trains may replace the wheel as a major component of train travel in the future. Instead of using steel wheels on conventional train tracks, Maglev trains float over a U-shaped or T-shaped track called a guideway. Magnets on the bottom of the train and on the floor of the guideway push in opposition to each other, thereby "floating" the train. Electric current is applied to special coils in the sides of the guideway that create other magnetic fields to push and pull the train along the track. Since Maglev trains float on a cushion of air, there is very little friction. This allows the trains to travel at speeds of more than 300 miles per hour (480 kmh), twice as fast as many steel-wheeled commuter trains.[5] The inventors even envision Maglev ramps one day shooting spacecraft into flight.

of muscle mass and bone density, in addition to other physical problems. A yearlong trip to Mars in zero gravity would compound these effects.

The earliest designers of space stations, in the 1940s and 1950s, acknowledged the need for artificial gravity. To create the effect of gravity where none was present, they envisioned constructing the stations in the shape of a large, three-story wheel. A power source would rotate the wheel once every 22 seconds to simulate one-third of the gravity experienced on Earth.[3] Although such designs were not used for the ISS, with longer trips into space now being considered, the old plans have been reviewed and revised to address current needs. Most of the configurations are very large and would house 12 to 50 people.[4] A station design called Nautilus-X, proposed in 2011 by a team of professionals from NASA, academia, and space-related industries, would carry six people and use existing

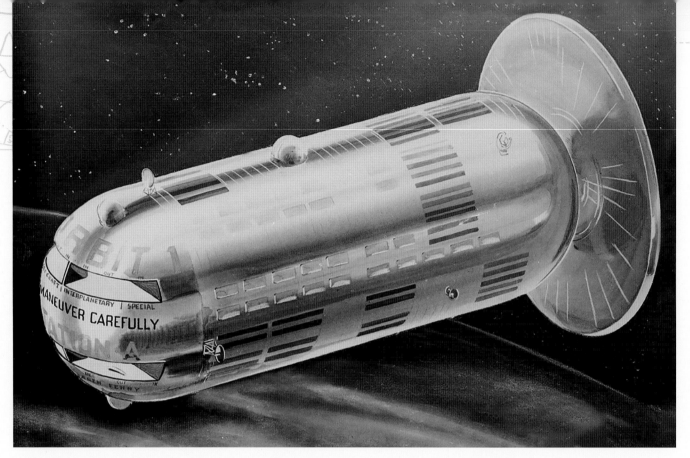

This space station, designed in 1956 by Darrell Romick, a scientist at the Goodyear Aircraft Company, features a giant gravity wheel at its base that would have been 1,500 feet (460 m) in diameter and nearly one mile (1.6 km) in circumference.

technology for building it in space.[6] Nautilus-X looks similar to the current ISS with one difference: it has a big inflatable donut in the middle—a gravity-simulating wheel.

Tightening government budgets may halt these long-distance space initiatives. However, hotel magnate Robert Bigelow, who has his own vision of hotels in orbit, owns the company developing the inflatable space material that would be used in the donut. These hotels would need artificial gravity, too. Private enterprise might lead the way to future long-range space travel.

From the day the first wheeled vehicle carried goods or people from one place to another, it opened up the world through travel. Wheeled vehicles and farm equipment fed nations. Wheeled machines made tasks simpler and helped workers be more productive, giving them time to pursue education, enjoy leisure time, and eventually become members of the new middle class. Wheels also contributed to the deadliness of wars, facilitated social, economic, and political change, and polluted the environment while using vast quantities of natural resources. Wheeled inventions changed the world and will continue to affect life on Earth and beyond for the foreseeable future.

THE BIONIC WHEEL

Due to improvements in modern medicine, injured people have a much greater chance of surviving a potentially life-ending loss of a limb. One of the downsides of surviving these terrible wounds is learning to live with and use prosthetic limbs. Miniature wheels, gears, and pulleys are helping bionic parts operate better. Companies such as Touch Bionics and the Biomechatronics Group are creating more efficient, powerful, and useful bionic parts, particularly for injured veterans returning from the wars in Iraq and Afghanistan.

THE NEXT
GENERATION: OMNI WHEELS

C an a car be made to pivot like an office chair and roll sideways into a parking spot? That was the question Stephen Killough of the Oak Ridge National Laboratory asked in the early 1990s. According to one science writer, his solution, the Omnidirectional Holonomic Platform (OHP), is "technically sweet, mathematically elegant, and visually discombobulating."[7] *Omnidirectional* means that something can move in any direction, and *holonomic,* when used in robotics, means that a device can move freely within the one-, two-, or three-dimensional space in which it operates.

The OHP developed by Killough and Francois Pin consists of six semispherical wheels that allow an object to move in any direction by rotating, somewhat

The advantage of omni wheels is that they roll forward and backward like normal wheels, but they can also slide sideways with a minimal amount of friction.

The Mecanum wheel, introduced in 1973, is also known as the Ilon wheel after its Swedish inventor, Bengt Ilon. Ilon invented the wheel while working for Mecanum AB, a Swedish company. He sold his patent to the US Navy in the 1980s.

like the casters on an office chair. The three pairs of wheels are mounted on a round platform and are configured in a Y formation, with each pair driven by its own motor. Many variations of the omni wheel are now in use, including the Mecanum omni wheel, which consists of oblong rollers set at an angle around the outside of a hub. Omni wheels are suitable for robots, forklifts, wheelchairs, and other wheeled devices that need to operate in narrow and crowded spaces, such as factories, warehouses, and hospitals.

DATE OF INVENTION

ca. 3500 BCE

KEY PLAYERS

The inventor (or multiple inventors) of the wheel and the earliest wheeled vehicles and machines are not known. It is only since the advent of recorded history that individual inventors can be identified.

▶ Englishman Thomas Savery builds the first steam engine; Scotsman James Watt perfects it.

▶ Richard Trevithick, an Englishman, builds the first successful steam locomotive.

▶ American Robert Fulton builds the first practical waterwheel steamboat.

▶ Englishman James Starley creates the tangent-spoke wheel; his nephew John Kemp Starley designs the first modern bicycle.

▶ German Karl Benz builds a four-wheeled car with a gasoline engine.

▶ American Henry Ford releases the first mass-produced automobile.

KEY TECHNOLOGIES

▶ Pottery wheel

▶ Early wheeled vehicles with axles and bearings

▶ Waterwheels and windmills

▶ Steam-powered machines for agricultural, industrial, and military use

- Transportation innovations (bicycles, trains, airplanes, outer-space vehicles, and cars and trucks)

- Entertainment and information uses (recording technology and computers)

EVOLUTION AND UPGRADES

The wheel and axle is a simple machine that operates the same today as when it was first introduced early in human history. What has changed with time is how it is used in combination with other devices (such as with gears, pulleys, cranks, etc.), what materials it is made of, and to which devices it is attached. The most significant upgrade to the wheel has been its power source, evolving from human and animal power, to water, wind, steam, electricity, solar, and fossil fuels.

IMPACT ON SOCIETY

From the beginning, wheeled vehicles have given people more mobility and hauling power. They allow farmers and merchants to move more food and goods over greater distances, spreading people and ideas across continents. They also contribute to making wars more deadly. Wheel-using machines save time and labor. They give people time for leisure, school, and the arts. Wheel-using machines contribute to pollution and have shifted wealth from small farms and craftspeople to large agribusiness, banks, and manufacturing industries. By making global travel possible on a broad scale, wheels have facilitated the mixing of cultures and people.

QUOTE

"The mechanic should sit down among levers, screws, wedges, wheels, etc. like a poet among the letters of the alphabet, considering them as the exhibition of his thoughts; in which a new arrangement transmits a new idea to the world."

—*Robert Fulton, inventor of the first practical steamboat*

GLOSSARY

armament

Military weapons used to fight a war.

asphalt

A sticky, black mixture of petroleum compounds; mixed with sand and gravel to make roads.

bloomers

Full, loose trousers gathered at the knee formerly worn by women for athletic activities.

catapult

An ancient spring-loaded weapon used for throwing large rocks.

curricle

A light, two-wheeled vehicle pulled by two horses.

domesticate

To tame an animal.

gig

A light, two-wheeled, one-horse carriage.

Goth

A member of a Germanic people group that overran the Roman Empire in the early centuries of the Christian era.

incline

A slanting surface or slope.

latitude

The distance north or south of the equator measured in degrees up to 90 degrees.

mainframe

A large, high-speed computer that supports multiple workstations and/or peripheral devices.

pictograph

An ancient or prehistoric drawing or painting on a cave wall.

piston

The part of an engine that moves up and down inside a tube and causes other parts of the engine to move.

pneumatic

Air-filled.

sheathe

To cover something with another material, usually to protect it.

sledge

A small vehicle with a flat bottom or runners.

steppe

A large, flat area of grassland characterized by very few trees.

stylus

A small, pointed piece of metal that touches the surface of a record to produce sound.

tangent

A straight line that touches, but does not intersect, a curved line or surface.

yoke

A bar or frame attached to the heads or necks of two animals so they can pull a heavy load.

SELECTED BIBLIOGRAPHY

Bunch, Bryan, and Alexander Helleman. *The History of Science and Technology: A Browser's Guide to the Great Discoveries, Inventions, and the People Who Made Them, from the Dawn of Time to Today.* Boston: Houghton, 2004. Print.

Carlisle, Rodney. *Scientific American Inventions and Discoveries: All the Milestones in Ingenuity— from the Discovery of Fire to the Invention of the Microwave Oven.* Hoboken, NJ: Wiley, 2004. Print.

Goddard, Jolyon, ed. *National Geographic Concise History of Science & Invention: An Illustrated Time Line.* Washington, DC: National Geographic, 2009. Print.

Wei, James. *Great Inventions That Changed the World.* Hoboken, NJ: Wiley, 2012. Print.

FURTHER READINGS

Challoner, Jack, ed. *1001 Inventions That Changed the World.* Hauppauge, NY: Barron's, 2009. Print.

Gottlieb, Joan S. *Wonders of Science: Matter, Motion, and Machines.* Orlando, FL: Steck-Vaughn, 2004. Print.

Penn, Robert. *It's All About the Bike: The Pursuit of Happiness on Two Wheels.* New York: Bloomsbury, 2010. Print.

WEBSITES

To learn more about Essential Library of Inventions, visit **booklinks.abdopublishing.com**. These links are routinely monitored and updated to provide the most current information available.

FOR MORE INFORMATION

For more information on this subject, contact or visit the following organizations:

Mid-America Windmill Museum

732 South Allen Chapel Road
Kendallville, IN 46755
260-347-2334
http://www.midamericawindmillmuseum.org

This museum displays 52 windmills on its grounds. Exhibits, video presentations, guided tours, and a library tell the story of wind power in the United States from its inception to the present day.

Smithsonian Institution *America on the Move* Exhibit

The National Museum of American History, Behring Center
Fourteenth Street & Constitution Avenue, NW
Washington, DC 20001
202-663-1000
http://amhistory.si.edu/onthemove/visit

This ongoing exhibit uses multimedia technology and other theatrical techniques to show visitors how ships, trains, trucks, and automobiles shaped American history. The museum features a restored 1903 Winton, the first car driven across the United States.

Wheels O' Time Museum

1710 West Woodside Drive
Dunlap, IL 61525
309-243-9020
http://www.wheelsotime.org

This museum, located near Peoria, features items from 50 to 100 years ago relating to transportation, home life, farming, and entertainment.

SOURCE NOTES

Chapter 1. The Wheel

1. Stephen B. Goddard. *Colonel Albert Pope and His American Dream Machine: The Life and Times of a Bicycle Tycoon Turned Automotive Pioneer.* Jefferson, NC: McFarland, 2008. Print. 10.

2. "The History of Starley Bikes." *Starley.* Starley Bikes, n.d. Web. 9 Nov. 2014.

3. "Wheel." *Etymonline.com.* Online Etymology Dictionary, 2014. Web. 26 Nov. 2014.

4. "Robert Fulton." *Todayinsci.* Today in Science History, n.d. Web. 10 Dec. 2014.

5. Molly Oldfield and John Mitchinson. "QI: Quite Interesting Facts about Wheels." *Telegraph.* Telegraph Media Group, 19 June 2013. Web. 26 Nov. 2014.

6. Ibid.

7. "Facts about Ferris Wheels and the 10 Tallest." *The Big Story.* Associated Press, 27 Sept. 2012. Web. 27 Nov. 2014.

Chapter 2. Why the Wheel?

1. "Ice, Snow, and Glaciers: The Water Cycle." *USGS.* US Geological Survey, 19 Dec. 2014. Web. 12 Feb. 2015.

2. Jolyon Goddard, ed. *National Geographic Concise History of Science & Invention: An Illustrated Time Line.* Washington, DC: National Geographic, 2009. Print. 35.

Chapter 3. Creating the First Wheel

1. David W. Anthony. *The Horse, the Wheel and Language: How Bronze-Age Riders from the Eurasian Steppes Shaped the Modern World.* Princeton, NJ: Princeton UP, 2007. Print. 67–69.

2. "Carriages." *The Official Website of the British Monarchy.* The Royal Household, n.d. Web. 12 Feb. 2015.

3. Trevor I. Williams. *A History of Invention: From Stone Axes to Silicon Chips.* New York: Checkmark, 2000. Print. 63.

Chapter 4. Early Wheeled Machines

1. Rodney Carlisle. *Scientific American Inventions and Discoveries: All the Milestones in Ingenuity—from the Discovery of Fire to the Invention of the Microwave Oven.* Hoboken, NJ: Wiley, 2004. Print. 144.

2. Jolyon Goddard, ed. *National Geographic Concise History of Science & Invention: An Illustrated Time Line.* Washington, DC: National Geographic, 2009. Print. 85.

3. Chris Woodford. "Pulleys." *ExplainThatStuff. com.* Explain That Stuff!, 25 May 2014. Web. 13 Nov. 2014.

4. Rodney Carlisle. *Scientific American Inventions and Discoveries: All the Milestones in Ingenuity—from the Discovery of Fire to the Invention of the Microwave Oven.* Hoboken, NJ: Wiley, 2004. Print. 103.

Chapter 5. Revolution on Wheels

1. Jolyon Goddard, ed. *National Geographic Concise History of Science & Invention: An Illustrated Time Line.* Washington, DC: National Geographic, 2009. Print. 145.

2. Joseph R. Conlin. *The American Past: A Survey of American History. Volume II: Since 1865.* Boston: Wadsworth, Cengage, 2013. Print. 564.

3. Rodney Carlisle. *Scientific American Inventions and Discoveries: All the Milestones in Ingenuity—from the Discovery of Fire to the Invention of the Microwave Oven.* Hoboken, NJ: Wiley, 2004. Print. 274.

Chapter 6. Wheeled Vehicles Speed Up

1. James A. Henretta, Rebecca Edwards, and Robert O. Self. *America: A Concise History. Volume 2: Since 1865.* Boston: Bedford/St. Martin's, 2012. Print. 495.

2. Jolyon Goddard, ed. *National Geographic Concise History of Science & Invention: An Illustrated Time Line.* Washington, DC: National Geographic, 2009. Print. 157.

3. Ibid. 218.

4. Megan Gambino. "A Salute to the Wheel." *Smithsonian.com.* Smithsonian Magazine, 17 June 2009. Web. 29 Oct. 2014.

5. Donald Cardwell. *Wheels, Clocks, and Rockets.* New York: Norton, 2001. Print. 368.

6. Rodney Carlisle. *Scientific American Inventions and Discoveries: All the Milestones in Ingenuity—from the Discovery of Fire to the Invention of the Microwave Oven.* Hoboken, NJ: Wiley, 2004. Print. 62.

7. Ibid. 253.

8. Bernard Pipkin, D. D. Trent, Richard Hazlett, and Paul Bierman. *Geology and the Environment.* Belmont, CA: Brooks/Cole Cengage Learning, 2011. Print. 532.

9. "On the Road to 'Sweet' Tires Made with a More Sustainable Process." *ACS Chemistry for Life.* American Chemical Society, 24 Mar. 2010. Web. 15 Mar. 2015.

Chapter 7. Modern Wheels

1. "USA Roller Sports." *Team USA*. United States Olympic Committee, n.d. Web. 3 Dec. 2014.

2. "IBM 350 Disk Storage Unit." *ibm.com*. IBM, n.d. Web. 12 Feb. 2015.

3. Ibid.

4. "Computer Memory." *Encyclopædia Britannica*. Encyclopædia Britannica, 2014. Web. 3 Dec. 2014.

5. "This Day in History: October 12." *History.com*. A&E Television Networks, n.d. Web. 5 Feb. 2015.

6. "Cunard Transatlantic Cruises." *Cruise Transatlantic*. Cunard Line, n.d. Web. 5 Feb. 2015.

7. *BritishAirways.com*. British Airways, n.d. Web. 12 Feb. 2015.

8. Karl Tate. "Distances Driven on Other Worlds (Infographic)." *Space.com*. Space.com, 24 Jan. 2013. Web. 3 Dec. 2014.

9. Rodney Carlisle. *Scientific American Inventions and Discoveries: All the Milestones in Ingenuity—from the Discovery of Fire to the Invention of the Microwave Oven*. Hoboken, NJ: Wiley, 2004. Print. 287.

10. Gendy Alimurung. "Movie Studios Are Forcing Hollywood to Abandon 35 mm Film." *LA Weekly*. LA Weekly, 12 Apr. 2012. Web. 3 Dec. 2014.

11. Nathan Naylor. "NHTSA Data Confirms Traffic Fatalities Increased in 2012." *NHTSA.gov*. National Highway Traffic Safety Administration, 14 Nov. 2013. Web. 1 Dec. 2014.

12. "It Will Help Save Our Auto Industry." *New York Times*. New York Times, 25 July 1982. Web. 5 Feb. 2015.

13. Rodney Carlisle. *Scientific American Inventions and Discoveries: All the Milestones in Ingenuity—from the Discovery of Fire to the Invention of the Microwave Oven*. Hoboken, NJ: Wiley, 2004. Print. 429–430.

14. Kelly Aspen. "The History of the Travel Trailer." *Trails.com*. Trails.com, n.d. Web. 3 Dec. 2014.

15. "Growth of Skateboarding and BMX." *SPAUSA.org*. Skate Park Association International, n.d. Web. 5 Feb. 2015.

Chapter 8. The Wheel Rolls On

1. Stephen Edelstein. "Polaris Airless Tires Go on Sale." *Motor Authority*. High Gear Media, 18 Nov. 2013. Web. 5 Feb. 2015.

2. Ed Grabianowski. "How the Tweel Airless Tire Works." *Howstuffworks.com*. How Stuff Works, n.d. Web. 3 Dec. 2014.

3. "IMAX Space Station Educator's Resource Guide." Lockheed Martin in cooperation with NASA, n.d. Web. 12 Feb. 2015.

4. Richard Hollingham. "The Rise and Fall of Artificial Gravity." *bbc.com*. BBC, 21 Jan. 2013. Web. 5 Dec. 2014.

5. Kevin Bonsor. "How Maglev Trains Work." *Howstuffworks.com*. How Stuff Works, n.d. Web. 4 Dec. 2014.

6. Richard Hollingham. "The Rise and Fall of Artificial Gravity." *bbc.com*. BBC, 21 Jan. 2013. Web. 5 Dec. 2014.

7. "1997 Discover Awards: Automotive & Transportation: Cleaner Than Air." *Discover*. Discover Magazine, 1 July 1997. Web. 5 Feb. 2015.

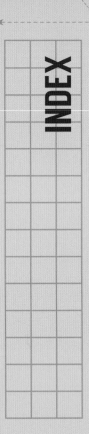

INDEX

About the Author

Melissa Higgins writes fiction and nonfiction for children and young adults. Two of her novels for struggling readers, *Bi-Normal* and *I'm Just Me,* won silver medals in the Independent Publisher (IPPY) Book Awards. Higgins's nearly 40 nonfiction titles range from character development and psychology to history and science. Before becoming a full-time writer, she worked as a school counselor and had a private counseling practice. When she is not writing, Higgins enjoys hiking and taking photographs in the Arizona desert, where she lives with her husband.

About the Consultant

John Hoard is associate research scientist in the Lay Auto Lab at the University of Michigan.